THE ACROPOLIS

GERHART RODENWALDT

THE ACROPOLIS

PHOTOGRAPHED BY WALTER HEGE

OXFORD
BASIL BLACKWELL
1957

First Edition 1930 Second Edition 1957

Printed in West Germany

CONTENTS

Plan of the Acropolis Pages 56-57; Table of Plates Page 59-61

The numbers at the inner margins refer to the Plates, those marked by "Pl." to the Plates in the Text.

INTRODUCTION

When Lord Elgin first exhibited the sculptures of the Parthenon in London, a chosen few realised that here was a great event. "I felt" wrote a young painter, "as if a divine revelation had stirred me to the depths of my being, and I knew that these works would at last rouse the art of Europe from its long sleep in darkness." But the power of "classicism" was too great to be immediately overthrown by a contact with classical art. It is true that Wilhelm von Humboldt, though more moved by words and ideas than by form, saw with amazing insight the importance of the Elgin marbles, and wrote of them: "Their main characteristics will always be nobility, vigour and plenitude of life. Compared with these works of art all others, even the most beautiful, seem poor, stiff and insignificant." In front of the originals he realised the inadequacy of a cast. Yet even he admired the "calm and candour" of Thorwaldsen's "Hope" which he purchased shortly afterwards at the desire of his wife, and which we, though still admiring, realise to be so far from conforming to the precepts of true classical art.

Even those who, like Goethe and Humboldt, were momentarily aware of the splendour of antique sculpture, turned back to the clear but subdued light of classicism. The artists of the time were astonishingly blind. Canova and Thorwaldsen felt the beauty of the Greek originals, and fought valiantly on their behalf, not so much for their own sakes as because they thought to find here the expression of their aspirations. They remained unaware of the great gulf that yawned between them. It was not, therefore, through lack of piety or through overwhelming conceit that Thorwaldsen undertook to restore the sculptures from the Aeginetan pediments, or that the fantasy of Schinkel would have made of the Acropolis a castle in the romantic tradition. It was from an excess admiration, a desire to give a new lease of life to these broken relics of antiquity.

Contemporary scholarship failed lamentably to realise the importance of the event. Though one of its most distinguished exponents declared that the history of art had found a new rallying-point, and a standard of values which would endure for ever, his conviction remained purely theoretical. Few were moved by it, and the value of imitative art, whether contemporary or Roman, was not questioned. There was no Winckelmann, sensitive to the beauty of the Greek originals, and capable of conveying his impression to his contemporaries. Even to-day classicism is not vanquished, and still, in the domain of plastic art, prevents immediate contact with the most important period of Greek sculpture. It is true that the idea which made of classical art a model to be copied at all costs, an ideal which was a source of inspiration to our ancestors, but a heavy burden to their immediate successors, has given way to the recognition of it as a perfect expression of European culture, which cannot again be achieved. We can now approach it free from all servility, to find in it incomparable pleasure and creative inspiration; though it is not to be denied that most people, accustomed as they are to the manifold art of the present day, find the archaic, the baroque and the later classical style more easily accessible than the true classic period. For the best classical art demands for its appreciation an inner harmony which must be attained before one can approach it in the right spirit. Yet an understanding of the classical art of the fifth and fourth centuries is absolutely necessary to an understanding of Greek art in general.

It has been said, and not without reason, that a modern Winckelmann would take as his starting point for the discovery of the Hellenic genius not art, the morphe, but philosophy, the logos. He who aspires to a complete understanding of the soul of Greece must travel by this road, for the contemplation of pure form does not lead one easily to the inner fastnesses. It is even more necessary that we should comprehend the spiritual soil from which sprang this flower of Greek art when we realise that, although so much of it is still accessible to us, we must for ever remain strangers to the greater part of classical antiquity. Even he whose eye is accustomed to the form and whose mind is attuned to the perception of Greek art cannot without difficulty appreciate at its true value a Greek temple or piece of sculpture. Hardly anything remains to us in its original setting, and we are apt too easily to supply by our imagination all that is lacking. The museums of western Europe are still under the influence of classicism. For the most part their treasures are Roman copies; figures designed to stand alone are incorporated into a scheme of decoration, and we are only just beginning to separate the copies from the originals and to assign to each piece its true value. And even the masterpieces seem dull and lifeless in the heavy atmosphere of our museums, deprived of that vital element for which and in which they were created – the clear light of Attica.

"The sensation of light" wrote a poet keenly sensitive to the beauty of antiquity, (Rudolf G. Binding: *Erlebtes Leben*) "is the most penetrating, most lasting sensation one can experience in Greece. Without this light neither Greece, nor her art, nor her Gods, nor her people would have been possible. Only in such an atmosphere could they have existed. It is not so much light as an infinite transparency. No man can say what its colour is. It is the very air which these stones breathe. . . . It is all clarity, all precision, it hates secrecy. The land lies fair and smiling before us and the air delights in nakedness. It makes everything simple, joyful, confident, clear."

If it is true that the time has come to liberate classical art from the confusion of classicism, then a renaissance of Greek monumental art can only be achieved after contemplation of the originals in the land which gave them being. Classical art has properties in common with the classicism which is its imitation. The subordination of the parts to the unity of the whole can be equally well understood from a cast in a museum. So can the harmony between the primary forms of the creative instinct, which have been variously defined as abstraction and representation, utilisation and imitation of nature, the form imposed and the form received. Proportion, harmony, clarity, and nobility distinguish the best works of classicism. But true classical art demands more than this, which a mediocre talent can attain by a judicious use of its opportunities. The strength of classical art lies in the restraint of profusion, the subjection of force to will. Behind the harmony of form is apparent the violence and passion which must lie at the heart of all truly great works of art. But the masterpieces of Greek art can only come to life under Greek skies, and the flower of this art is the Acropolis, with its buildings and their sculptural ornamentation, which a kindly destiny has preserved to us. Here, gleaming in immaculate marble, the essential forms of monumental architecture show to perfection, in that purity and simplicity of line which was only possible at this time, free from the violence and brutality of archaic and baroque art. He who, wandering on the Acropolis, feels himself penetrated by the wind of the spirit of this great art, finds and knows himself. Anatole France, to one who asked him the why and wherefore of his travels, replied: "When I wish to become a better man, I go to Greece."

No painter has been able to reproduce the unique atmosphere of the Acropolis, for since the rediscovery of these buildings, no phase of art has completely solved the problem of the reconciliation of clarity and colour, force and delicacy. Casts can render only the lifeless form. But photography, which has wrongly been considered a purely objective form of reproduction, can, at the sacrifice of colour reduced to a play of light and shadow, present form in its surroundings. Yet even photography meets with almost insurmountable difficulties, as much from the brilliancy of the light as from the violent foreshortening of objects. In the plates contained in this volume an artist has endeavoured to seize the essential. The detail of the sculpture is thrown up by the clear light, and against a dark background the marble columns gleam as in reality they gleam against the deep blue of the sky. A few views from the Acropolis Museum complete the photographs taken on the spot. They are presented here in an effort to help others towards an understanding of Greek art in its reality, that is, in its luminous vitality.

ACROPOLIS

Among the outcrops of rock which run beside and across the Attic plain, there are others higher and more striking than the Acropolis. But it was not chosen for its great destiny on account of its picturesqueness, but because of the suitability of its shape and position. The flat top of the enormous calcareous rock, which falls sharply away on three sides and can only be ascended by a steep path to the narrow western peak, seemed predestined to carry a fortress and a sanctuary. Now, as in classical times, it rises above the tumult of the town, bearing high up into the clear air the temples of the sacred precinct, an immense and firm foundation for the most beautiful edifices ever raised by the hand of man. Only on the west side is it connected by a natural bridge with the surrounding hills. On the other sides the ever-growing town, stretching out over the plain, presses close to its base. In the same way in classical times the town grouped itself round the Acropolis. The houses were low, and neither domes nor towers rivalled the majesty of the holy temples. Modern Athens, unlike many other towns of to-day, has been most restrained in her new buildings. No obtrusive modern architecture distracts one's attention, and as in olden times the Acropolis still reigns supreme. But we see the Acropolis with other eyes than the men of ancient Athens. For us, too, it is a sanctuary, but a sanctuary of aesthetic and historic interest, while for them it was a religious centre and a symbol of political power. If we wish to understand it in its entirety we must endeavour to visualise it under this aspect. The changes of the modern world make it difficult for us to recapture the spirit of the time. Even our very vision is different from that of classical Men. We see the Acropolis and its buildings as part of the surrounding landscape. From the hills around we see it rising above the town, white against a background of blue sea, or overtopped by Lycabettus and the monastery on its summit, or by the white slopes of Mount Pentelicus. The west wall rises up, towering above the chalk foundation and the green pine wood. As we climb the south slope, the jagged lines of the white marble ruins, rising from the bluish rock between the brown arches of the Roman temple, gleam against a deep blue sky. There is an exciting contrast between the rock formations of the stronghold and the marble buildings of the temple. The cliffs are formed of irregular outcrops of limestone whose bluish violet colour is shot through with red veins. In different lights, and according to the degree of humidity, the colour varies from grey-blue to violet and red. On this sombre, rude foundation rise the temples, warm with the golden tinge that Pentelic marble takes from weathering, harmonious with the sweep of rhythmic lines. From the fact that this contrast strikes us, and more forcibly every time we visit the Acropolis, we can judge of the difference between what we see and what the Athenian saw. Accustomed for so long to the modern conception of a landscape, we consider the temple and the rock as a picturesque unity. To us the contrast between form and colour is like two voices, each singing its own **part**, but harmoniously blending. The Greek heard only one voice, that of art. The form alone touched him; he was indifferent to Nature. For him this contrast between the ruggedness of nature and the perfection of man's handiwork held a more profound meaning. On the steps of the Parthenon he felt perhaps as Sophocles felt, when he wrote at the time of its construction:

"Many mighty things there are, but nothing is mightier than man."

The contrast between the whiteness of the marble and the dark colour of the rock helps us also to appreciate the Greek attitude, and therefore those pictures are particularly welcome which convey this contrast. There are other antique temples built of limestone, which now seem an integral part of the surrounding country, as if they had grown from the ground they stand on. When they were built, however, a dazzlingly white coat of plaster served to detach them from their surroundings.

The Greek isolated the work of art, seeing it as a whole, complete in itself. For this reason the buildings on the Acropolis are not designed in any relation to each other, but as separate units. The Parthenon, placed on the highest point, dominates the whole, but the Erechtheum, the Propylaea, and even the little Temple of Athena Nike stand independently beside it, absolutely self-contained. In this way the Acropolis differs from a mediaeval fortified castle, where house and chapel seemed part of the background with which they were so intimately connected, and where all the lines ran upward until they finally culminated in a high and solitary tower, rising into the sky.

In early times the interior of each building, too, was more independent of the scenery than it is to-day. Now one can see the sea, and the islands of Salamis and Aegina, and, across the town lying below in the plain, the green banks of the Cephisus. One can follow the line of hills which lead away to Eleusis, take in the marble quarries of Mount Pentelicus and enjoy the changing colours of Mount Hymettos. In antiquity one could only catch a glimpse of the sea from the terrace of the Nike temple, which stood directly in front of the entrance; high walls hid the town and the surrounding country. Once through the Propylaea, one found oneself in a sanctuary shut off from the rest of the world. Above the temples and the numerous bronze and marble statues stretched a vast expanse of sky, and only a few distant mountain tops showed above the great walls.

It was only after a long and chequered career, at about the time of the building of the Parthenon, that the Acropolis became a sacred precinct; but the goddess of the citadel was worshipped here from the earliest times, for from her, Athena, the city received its name. The cult of this warrior maiden, armed with spear and sword, was perhaps instituted here even before the Greeks took possession of the country, and it survived all the stress and turmoil of race migrations. The Acropolis was the obvious place of refuge for the inhabitants of the Attic plain, possibly the habitation of their rulers, and it was therefore natural that the goddess of the tribe should have her sanctuary here. Usually a cult remains faithful to the place with which it is first associated. The time-honoured objects of veneration, in historic times, were inside and near the present site of the Erechtheum. According to the old legend, Poseidon struck the rock with his trident and a salt spring gushed out; then Athena, under the eyes of King Cecrops, planted the first olive-tree in the rock itself, and was proclaimed patroness of the city. There, by the marks of the trident, the salt spring, the tomb of Cecrops and the olive-tree, was the primitive centre of worship. There was no temple, no idol, and only a wall separated the small precinct with its sacred objects from the houses which huddled together, covering the face of the rock. When, in the second half of the second millennium, Mycenaean civilisation reigned supreme in Greece, the Acropolis became the home of the king. The principal palace was evidently built immediately beside the sacred enclosure, a little to the south, on the spot where later stood the early temple of Athena, and it seems probable that a temple attached to the palace was dedicated to the worship of the patroness of the city. The whole of the Acropolis was surrounded by enormous Cyclopean walls, the greater part of which still stand to-day, and a strongly fortified gate guarded the entrance. At this time Greeks of Ionic stock were already established in Attica, and they remained there when, towards the end of the second millennium, a flourishing civilisation decayed and foundered in the storms of the Doric migration.

The tradition which made of the Acropolis the city dated from the early centuries of the first millennium. Whilst in the Mycenaean epoch probably a lower town had grown up, the city then rose on the rock again. Miserable huts built of mud bricks and separated by narrow lanes may have covered the hill's surface and its slopes to the West and South. One rather larger building served as a dwelling-place for the king. The sacred precinct of Athena had survived and became crowded with altars and very simple votive offerings. Other gods, too, had their modest precincts here. Greek sanctuaries originally had no temple, but were merely strips of ground, usually planted with trees and surrounded by walls, and accessible by one door only. Sacrifices were made at an altar in the open air. It was only in the course of the seventh century, when the legendary kingdom was already extinct, that several small temples were built, of which the most important was that near the spring and the olive-tree, on the site of the old royal palace, whose territory was now incorporated into the sacred precinct. In this temple was venerated, along with the patroness of the city, the hero Erechtheus, born of the Attic soil, and chosen by Athena to be her priest and the ruler of her country.

The history of arts in Attica represents a contest between a passionate power of invention and a classic restraint. The beginning of monumental sculpture is later here than in Doric Peloponnese and on the Ionian Islands, but even the early works in marble have power to move us deeply. The first period of importance began between 590 and 560, when Solon, one of the seven sages of Greece, poet, statesman and philosopher, brought into being the constitutional state of Attica, sublime alliance of profound ethics with practical measure and so paved the way for the idea of a democracy. All that was achieved during these years was destroyed by later generations and by the Persian invasion; a few broken pieces of statuary in the Acropolis Museum are all that remains, and only in imagination can we reconstruct the aspect of the archaic Acropolis.

At this time there stood on the Acropolis, besides chapels and treasure-houses, great temples of whose cult we know very little. Their sculpture was of soft brown stone, painted in bright colours. Immense force, long restrained, expressed itself in statues and other objects of enormous dimensions. The old oriental motif of a fight between a lion and a bull was seized upon, and in Greek hands became a struggle between two elemental forces, the blind strength of the bull and the *Pl. 2* proud ferocity of the lion. On one of the oldest pediments a huge lioness has thrown a bull calf to the ground and is tearing it to pieces with her claws. Another later pediment, in the center of *Pl. 3* which two lions claw a bull, shows in its angles heroic subjects: Heracles is fighting with a Triton's *Pl. 4* rude power, while, on the other side, a Typhon strives with an unidentified figure. The shapes express the titanic nature of the struggle. The staring eyes, rounded cheeks, and the sensual curve of the red lips speak of a savage and almost overwhelming vitality. A classicist and perhaps even a classical artist would have found this art barbarous. The force behind it was indeed barbarous, but the will which restrained and dominated this barbarism more and more in every new piece of work was truly Greek.

The pediment which shows the fight of Heracles and the Triton was placed on the front of a temple which, towards the end of the Age of Solon, was erected to the honour of the goddess of the city and her protégé, Erechtheus. From the roof of the Parthenon one can trace quite clearly the plan of *Pl. 1* this temple, whose foundations can be seen on the flat space in front of the Erechtheum. A pillared

13

hall surrounded the cella of which the eastern end had been devoted to Athena, the western one to Erechtheus. Since, from the time of the Doric invasion, Attica had followed the fortunes of the civilisation of the Greek mainland, it is only to be expected that its architecture should be Doric. Here, as in the Peloponnesus where the Doric temple originated, simple limestone was used, covered with a gleaming white coat of plaster. The triglyphs and facets were painted black, the ornamentation and foliage red and blue. The brilliant colouring of the corona lessened the brutality of the contest on the triangular pediment. A gorgon in flight decorated the acroter. Her head was supposed to avert all evil from the sacred edifice.

Besides decorative sculpture, the Acropolis was strewn with votive figures, some of which were inside the temples, some on the ground outside. The worshippers who crowded to this holy place offered either a statue of the goddess or their own image. One of these has been discovered – the *Pl. 9* statue of a man bearing a calf on his shoulders, even as to-day in Greece the peasants come to the town at Easter carrying a lamb. The figure is that of a man tall and slim, with a frank and smiling countenance, in its noble virility a worthy expression of the joyful creative force of the time. But a certain stiffness and desire for symmetry still forbade absolute freedom of pose. It is a characteristic feature of Greek art, as of all European art, that it does not express itself in straight lines but in softly rounded curves.

After Solon came the tyranny of Peisistratus and his sons. Up till now the ancient civilisation had been closely connected with the Doric development of the mainland. Peisistratus endeavoured to transplant into Athens the kingly splendour of the Greek Orient. Ionic poets and artists came at his bidding, and by the resultant contact of Doric, Ionic, and autochthonous Attic influences, the ground was prepared for the final fusion of these elements which, a century later, produced the masterpieces of Athenian art.

Peisistratus began to erect a great Ionic temple to Zeus south of the Acropolis where later the Olympeium stood and left the temple of Athena undisturbed. The citadel, however, became *4* encumbered with votive offerings and statues, often placed on high columns, in which the later period of archaic Ionic art developed, on Attic soil, into a sort af elegant rococo. A number of graceful statues of young girls, which date from this time, have been recovered from the ruins of the Acropolis, the paint still discernible on them. These also must be seen in the brilliant Grecian sun- *Pl. 11, 12* light to be properly appreciated. Attic knights offered statues of themselves on horseback, or of their horses alone, broad-backed, long-legged animals with small hoofs and proud, expressive heads. It has been said with much truth that though these old artists may have made mistakes in the anatomy of a horse, they could interpret its soul, and may indeed claim to have discovered it.

14

By the side of this elegant **art**, which acts as it were an intermediary role, can be found works which in their weight reveal the striving forces of the creative genius of Attica. In the time of Peisistratus' sons the temple of Athena was re-erected. It was built of limestone, the material used for the main building, but the roof and the pediments were of marble. The East pediment, which originally held the combat of Heracles and the Triton, was given up to an even more imposing subject – the battle of the Gods and Giants, with Athena in the centre felling an enemy with a mighty blow. Her face has none oft the delicate beauty of the faces of the young girls referred to above. It has more gravity and sadness, in spite of the smile curving the lips. It is the natural transition to the severer and more dignified art of the last years before the Persian wars. Art, as well as Tragedy, which is just beginning to develop, is influenced by the new spirit of the time. The statue *Pl. 10* of a young man discovered on the Acropolis has a freer and more natural pose, a grave face with serious eyes. But we must remember that the beauty of this young body could not have been so marvellously rendered in marble had it not been for the mastery and technique of the Ionic craftsmen. In the head of a boy Attic gravity is allied with Ionic technique, influenced by Doric purity of form. The face is rendered amazingly lifelike by the remains of colours, without which one cannot imagine a Greek original, though classicism venerated pure white marble as the symbol of perfection. The hair was painted yellow, the lips and the edges of the eyelids red. The eyes were yellow with a black centre and rim. The head is truly representative of the generation which had the force to withstand the Persian wars, and emerge victorious from them.

The archaic Acropolis was burnt down by the Persians in 480 B.C. It is easy to understand how the Greeks, when they saw their sanctuaries destroyed by the barbarians, should have considered the possibility of leaving them in ruins in memory of the great struggle. But the necessity for continuing religious observances, and a natural desire for progress, soon made them realise that this was impracticable. During the fifty years between the Persian invasion and the outbreak of the Peloponnesian war Greek art developed with amazing rapidity to its final classical perfection, of which Greek Tragedy and the Acropolis are the supreme examples. In the fire not only the temples but all the profane buildings on the Acropolis had been destroyed. In the first moment of terror the Acropolis was surrounded by strongly fortified walls, but the ordinary buildings were not re-erected, and the whole of the Acropolis became a precinct sacred to the goddess Athena. When, after the erection of the Propylaea and the Parthenon, in the intervals of the Peloponnesian wars, the Nike Temple and the Erechtheum were perfected, the Acropolis took on the appearance that it has preserved through all vicissitudes until to-day. There were many small sanctuaries like that of Artemis Brauronia, but their buildings, which have since disappeared, had no artistic value. Year by year, however, the number of votive statues and inscriptions increased, covering all the available space with a confusion which would certainly have disconcerted us. Only one more temple was built on the Acropolis, when the citizens of Athens, desirous of thanking Augustus for his beneficence towards them, raised in his honour and that of the goddess Roma a graceful little monopteros on the east of the Parthenon, built in an Ionic style copied from the Erechtheum. With great discretion this elegant little building did not attempt to rival the great works of art which surrounded it.

The south slope was still to undergo great changes. On the western side of it was the Odeum, built by Pericles, and the sanctuary of Dionysus including the theatre where, from the beginning of the fifth century, the Greek tragedies were acted. All that remains of the Amphitheatre dates from the fourth century, while the stage is of an even later date. On a terrace in the middle of the south slope was the sanctuary of Asclepius and Hygieia, built in 420, an object of particular veneration to the ordinary citizens of the town. Further down Eumenes, King of Pergamum, built an enormous portico, and near it is the great Roman Odeum, once roofed in, which after 161 A. D. was dedicated by the rich orator, Herodes Atticus, to the memory of his wife Regilla. The decorative marble which covered its walls and arches has disappeared, and now it seems merely a part of the landscape above *3, 6, 7* which tower the gleaming classical buildings.

The steep rocks of the north slope, in whose caves Pan and Apollo were worshipped, have remained untouched until now. If we look over the wilderness of stones or across the poor streets towards where, after the Persian wars, the ruins of the old buildings were used in the construction of the walls, we probably still see exactly what was to be seen in the fifth century.

Athens and the Acropolis had already suffered many disasters when, towards the middle of the fifth century, A.D., the classical age came to an end with the removal of the Parthenos. The neoplatonic philosophers had fought valiantly here for paganism, and when Phidias's gold and ivory statue was removed from the Parthenon, the goddess appeared in a vision to Proclus the philosopher, in the form of a beautiful woman, and ordered him to prepare his house for her reception, "For the Mistress of Athens" she said, "desires to remain with you."

The disasters that overtook the town and the citadel from the end of antiquity to the Turkish conquest have been described at length by Gregorovius in his "History of Athens in the Middle Ages". In spite of the compassion we must feel in following the destinies of this city, so fallen from its high estate and almost forgotten for many centuries, we cannot help marvelling at the romantic and fantastic changes it underwent until its final liberation from Turkish rule. The Parthenon and the Erechtheum became Christian churches. After the Latin crusade of 1204 they became Roman churches, and the Propylaea became the residence of Frankish dukes. Here reigned, one after

16

1. View from the roof of the Parthenon towards the site of the early Temple of Athena

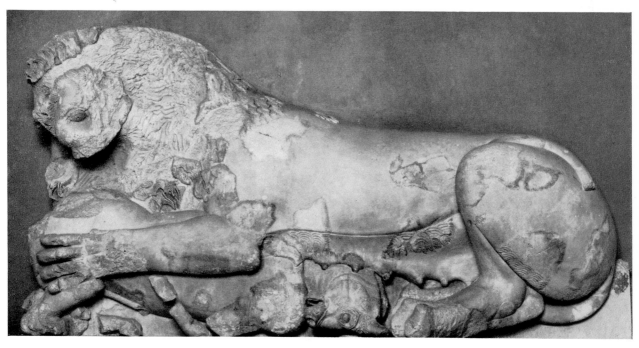

2. Lioness and young bull, from an early pediment

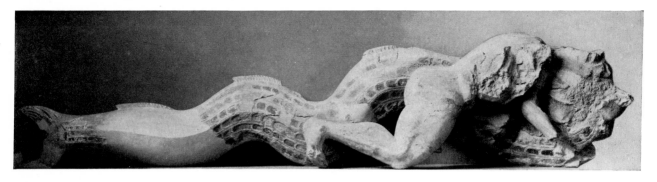

3. Herakles and Triton from the pediment of the early Temple of Athena

5. Parthenon. East pediment. Drawings attributed to Carrey

7. Parthenon. West pediment. Drawings attributed to Carrey

18

4. Typhon from the pediment of the early Temple of Athena

6. Parthenon. East pediment. Drawings attributed to Carrey

8. Parthenon. West pediment. Drawings attributed to Carrey

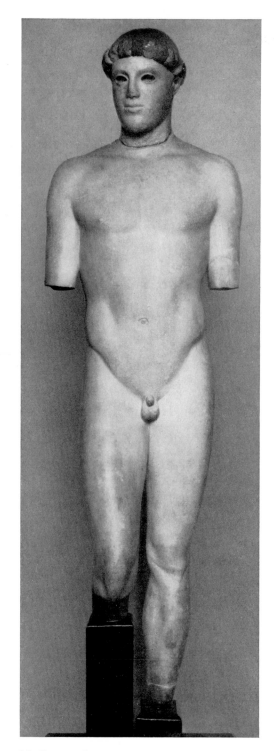

9. Man bearing sacrificial calf

10. Statue of young man.
(Early classical period.)

11. Female draped figure

12. Female draped figure

13. The Acropolis in 1670

VEDUTA DEL CAST: D'ACROPOLIS DALLA PARTE DI TRAMONTANA

14. Explosion of the Parthenon in 1687 (From a contemporary print by Fanelli in „Atene attica")

22

15. The Acropolis and the Frankish tower. From a contemporary sketch by the sculptor B. K. Heller, 1837

16. The Acropolis in the eighteenth century (From Stuart and Revett, Antiquities of Athens, 1841)

17. Early cast of slab V, West Frieze

18. Early cast of slab VIII, West Frieze

24

another, the Ducs de la Roche, Catalian mercenaries and the Florentine family of the Acciaioli. One branch of the Medici family settled in Athens and became Greek. The Middle Ages and Antiquity were strangely linked when knightly tournaments were held in front of the Parthenon, and commemorated by sketches scratched on the bases of its columns.

One relic of the Frankish epoch, the high tower erected near the Propylaea, remained standing until about the end of the last century. It was symbolic of the Middle Ages, and a prominent *Pl. 15* feature of all old pictures of the Acropolis. Rising up, solid and uncompromising, in the centre of the citadel, it became a rallying-point around which all the other buildings seemed grouped. It is astonishing how immediately, on the erection of this tower, the Acropolis assumed the appearance of a fortified mediaeval castle. After its destruction the single buildings regained their individuality. It is unfortunate that its disappearance should have destroyed for ever a reminder of a fascinating epoch, but the sacrifice was necessary if we were to restore the Acropolis of antiquity. Even in the picture it expresses, by the contrast, the spirit of antiquity.

After the Turkish conquest in 1458 the commandant of the citadel installed himself in the ducal *Pl. 13* palace, the Erechtheum became a harem and the Parthenon a mosque. Beside it rose a slender minaret. The admirably constructed marble edifices stood firm during all these upheavals, until in the seventeenth century a series of disastrous events dealt them a mortal blow. About 1645 the Propylaea, which were being used as a powder magazine, were struck by ligthning. In 1690 the Venetians, under Count Königsmarck, besieged the Acropolis. The Turks transported their powder to the Parthenon, in the hope that the Christians would spare this sacred building. But, we read in the *Pl. 14* report of a Hessian regiment, a Luneburg lieutenant "carried away by anger, went so far as to throw bombs against the temple." The subsequent explosion, which brought about the capitulation of the city, also destroyed the interior of the Parthenon, the whole of the roof and some of the sculptures of the pediments. Later on the Turks built a little mosque in the ruins. Houses and narrow streets *Pl. 16* covered the face of the rock, as in the days before the Persian wars. In 1833 the Turks finally evacuated the Acropolis. A year later Schinkel was given the task of planning a royal palace for the citadel. Happily his classicist Acropolis remained a project only. But, like the mediaeval castle, it provides an interesting contrast to the classical citadel. Schinkel had no intention of interfering with the ancient buildings. He planned to erect the palace on the lower east side, and its elevation was so low that the Parthenon would have towered above it, dominating it. But he would have liked to have brought the temple in line with the palace, and he planned to surround it by a symmetrical open space. Finally he tried to co-ordinate all the buildings into a coherent whole, and in order to effect this he introduced into his scheme gardens and groups of trees. He did not appear to realise that in

25

this way he would have destroyed the essential characteristic of the classical edifices, which stand isolated, without any connection with their surroundings.

After the evacuation of the Turks the fortress of the Acropolis was abandoned, and the citadel was given over to the archaeologists. They have had to fulfil a double task, that of studying it from an aesthetic and historical point of view, and that of making it once more a sanctuary. All traces of later and non-religious occupation were removed. Excavations have revealed the history of the citadel in archaic times. Soon after its liberation a German scholar reconstructed the temple of Athena Nike, whose fragments he discovered built into a Turkish bastion. In our time the Greek guardians of this European treasure-house have continued the work of restoration with the utmost conscientiousness and supreme tact. They have never actually rebuilt, but have contented themselves with replacing as far as possible in their original places the stones which strewed the ground, and, because of the excellence of the original construction, this could be carried out exactly. Just at a few unimportant points the buildings have been restored. The Erechtheum has been given its primitive form and aspect by the rebuilding of its walls, the east front of the Propylaea has been given back its entablature and a part of the pediment, while, in the west portico, a slender Ionic column once more supports the casket ceiling. Now, after much hard work, the fallen columns of the north *11* portico of the Parthenon have been raised, and in this way the peristyle has regained its original beauty. Finally the temple of Athena Nike has been restored to perfection by the Greek monument's *72* custodians.

"It is characteristic of the best works of antiquity and, I believe, of great art in general, that one cannot isolate one detail or one idea and say: This is the most beautiful. One must say it of the whole, for it is in its entirety that it is beautiful; the parts are the natural components of the whole." What Stifter says in "Nachsommer" of the statues in the Rosenhaus can be most truly applied to the Parthenon. A favourable providence has conserved to us a building which, in the intention of its creators, was to express the splendour of the most fortunate period in Greek history. Each part serves the harmony of the whole, and to the last chisel-stroke it was completed in accordance with the original plan.

When the Persians took the citadel the only sanctuary consecrated to the worship of Athena was the primitive temple which the Peisistratides had surrounded by a colonnade. Owing to the rapid political and intellectual development, pre-classical buildings were soon considered obsolete. Probably even before the Persian wars the sacred precinct had been enlarged on the south, towards the highest point of the rock; and by means of foundation walls the ground had been banked up to form a flat space on which a new and larger temple was begun. It was at first planned to build it in limestone, but it was actually started in marble. Beside this new temple, as was and is the habit in Greece, the old temple still stood. The fire destroyed what was finished and what was only begun, and in the subsequent confusion all plans had to give way before the necessity for defending the citadel. Themistocles turned Athens into a fortress and joined it to the Piraeus. On the Acropolis the cella of the ruined temple was roughly, restored to provide accommodation for worship. The fragments of other ruined buildings were used to strengthen the north wall and, after the naval battle of the Eurymedon, Cimon raised on the south of the Acropolis a great stone wall. Although the Acropolis was not originally intended to be a citadel, its position and shape made it the natural refuge in time of war or revolution, even in the days when it was definitely considered a sanctuary only. Before this great south wall was patched up by the Turks it must have appeared as an enormous socle for the temples above it.

What parts in the plan of the Parthenon must be attributed to political ideas, what to religious, what to artistic? The Greeks did not consider beauty as an end in itself. Everything on the citadel was an offering to the goddess, and its beauty was only the expression of religious sentiment. The creative force was so strong that it caused beautiful things to be put even in places where human eyes could not properly see and enjoy them. But this religious sentiment both in character and political ties differed from the religious sentiment which in the Middle Ages was responsible for the building of cathedrals and churches. We know nothing of the personal piety of such men as Pericles, Sophocles and Phidias, and can never know anything, because in antiquity there was not the interest in the individual that there is to-day. We can, however, conjecture that there existed, then as always, a naive and intimate piety, but it had nothing to do with the building of the Parthenon, nor with the gold and ivory statue which stood in it. The people probably held far dearer the old wooden image in the Erechtheum, or the sanctuary of Asclepius. When the Athenian looked at the Parthenon and its great statue he had not so much a sentiment of reverence as a feeling of pride in considering the goddess as the incarnation of the State and its power. Greek religion was pre-eminently a State religion. But it had no dogma, and knew no constraint. Religious opinion was a private and not a public matter. This explains the absence of a church, and of any official link between religion and art. The relation between religion and the State was limited to the exercise of ceremonial rites.

This cult has a peculiar significance when we consider the form of democracy which flourished in Athens under Pericles. The Athenian democracy had no responsible chief, representing in his person the State. This representation was embodied in the goddess, true sovereign of the land of Attica. The State treasure was kept in her temple, the stelae on which were inscribed all records of civic importance were dedicated to her, the feasts celebrated in her honour shone with magnificence, and in the documents she is the personification of power. So the goddess who had given her name to this city became its head to an even greater degree than later Saint Mark became of the Venetian republic. For this reason the building of the Parthenon must be considered as a political move on the part of the man who, towards the middle of the century, became in reality the head of the Athenian democracy. The end of the war and the consolidation of the state through "the authority of the first citizen", made possible by the form of democracy which was supreme in Attica, were the necessary preparatives to the great work of Athens as a civilising force during the short twenty years of the "age of Pericles". This is not the place to describe the glory, as well as the shame, of this time. It is, however, as well to remember that during the building of the Parthenon Sophocles produced his "Antigone" and Euripides his "Alcestis". It was decided to build the Parthenon immediately after the conclusion of peace with the Persians, and work began in 447. Other buildings were also being built at this time, but the temple which was to house the divinity of the State was also intended as a symbol of its power, and a proof of its glory for future generations. The best artists procurable were engaged on its decoration, and only the best materials were employed. The architect responsible for planning it was Ictinus, the best architect of his time. The gold and ivory statue was the work of Phidias, who had executed in the same materials the statue of Zeus at Olympia. The whole building, architecture and decorations included, was under the supervision of Phidias, who must have been an excellent organiser as well as a strong personality. This single supervision accounts for the harmony which reigns throughout the building. Pericles was a member of the commission appointed to construct the edifice, and it is most probable that Phidias talked over every point with him. Had Pericles a deep feeling for art which enabled him to bridge the gap between the aristocrat and the artisan, and to form a personal friendship with Phidias? Or did he consider art merely as a form of representation or even as a means of giving remunerative occupation to men of all classes? We know too little of him to be able to answer these questions definitely, though undoubtedly he possessed, together with great nobility of character and high ideals, the brain of a politician, and a power of making use of people in the right way. The unusual commission given to Phidias to supervise the building may perhaps be explained as an act of confidence in his ability, made at the particular request of Pericles.

There were temples larger than the Parthenon in Antiquity. The reason for its great importance is that, by a happy coincidence, the most powerful and ambitious builder of the time worked with the greatest artist, and this at the moment when classical art had reached the highest point of its development. Doric architecture might well have reached its culminating point in a smaller building, and decorative sculpture have produced its most beautiful work for a less extensive undertaking. But in this immense effort the creative genius of the time had unlimited opportunities for the employment of its faculties. To the gold and ivory statue of the goddess was added more sculptural decoration than had ever before been designed for a temple – 92 metopes, a frieze of about 176 yards in length and the figures of the pediments. The material used for the whole of the construction was Pentelic marble, whose delicacy permitted a technical perfection which could not have been achieved with any other stone. Plutarch spoke truly when he said that one should admire not only the majesty of the building and the beauty of its detail but also the rapidity of its construction. In ten years the building was roofed in, and the statue could be put in position. Six years later the sculptures of the pediments were finished. Only the acroteria were left for a later generation to construct.

Careful organisation was needed for the work to advance so quickly, an organisation extending to everything connected with it. This organisation is described by Plutarch. He gives a list of the materials which were used – stone, bronze, ivory, gold, ebony, cypress-wood – and of the craftsmen working on them – carpenters, sculptors, moulders, metal-workers, carvers in ivory, stonemasons, painters, and embroiderers; then of all those who were connected with the transport and handling of the materials – at sea, merchants, boatmen, and pilots; on land, carters and carriers, rope-makers, weavers, tanners, roadmakers, and workmen. Each of these services had working for it a crowd of labourers and odd-job men, and so all had their part in the work and in the prosperity which it brought about. The Acropolis, which was not yet covered with votive offerings, became a vast workshop for stonemasons and sculptors, whose work could be usefully combined since one brain governed this vast and complicated organisation. In the fervour of achievement, nobody troubled about conserving the remains of the older sculptures and buildings, and all traces of archaic art were lost in the debris which served as a foundation for the realisation of the ideals of this vigorous epoch.

The new building was built on a site where previously a big temple had been begun. This earlier building was to have been long and narrow, as was customary in early times, and would have had only six columns in front. The new building was calculated in the proportion of length and breadth which was later considered classic – eight columns in front and seventeen on each side. The sub-structure of the earlier building had to be widened, but its whole length was not needed. On its lowest level the temple measured 222 ft. by 102 ft. In the interior was a cella which opened back and front on a portico of six columns. The usual interior plan of a Doric temple consists of an oblong space with a prodomus in front of the principal entrance, and an opisthodomus behind, the latter merely for the sake of preserving the symmetry of the exterior. The dual purpose for which the Parthenon was built occasioned a different distribution of the rooms, which accounts for the back and front being alike. The east front belongs to the actual cella which covers the traditional length of 100 Attic feet. In other temples the sacred statues were usually housed in a room which had been constructed without reference to them. Here we can see the co-operation of the sculptor and the architect, endeavouring to bring into direct relation the room and the statue for which it was intended. Ictinus altered the traditional division, which gave one broad nave with two smaller naves on each side, and designed a room which should contain the statue and be surrounded by a peristyle. The statue was isolated by means of a balustrade. A gallery ran round the room, and two rows of columns one upon another supporting the casket ceiling divided the room vertically; their slenderness served to emphasise the enormous bulk of the statue. The gold and ivory of which the statue was composed gleamed in the warm light which entered by the great eastern door. Now that the divisions and partition walls have fallen, and only the west wall is still in position, we cannot

16, 17 imagine what the original effect of the room must have been. We can only admire the great door, and the beauty of the construction and workmanship of the wall.

It is impossible also for us to realise the impression that must have been produced on all who saw it by the gold and ivory statue. The small and altogether inferior copies which still exist cannot do it justice. An old statue of Athena which has been discovered on the Acropolis, and which follows probably a tradition unbroken from time immemorial, shows the goddess with one foot forward, a shield on her left arm and a lance in her right hand. In archaic times one liked to represent the godhead in action. The Athena who received from the people the name of Parthenos, Maiden, was a typical representation of the divinity in the first classical period, the rich and powerful sovereign of Attica. In a solemn and dignified attitude, clothed in splendid armour, holding in her right hand the statue of the goddess of victory, she stands ready to receive the homage of her people. Before her statue were crowned the victors of the Panathenaic games, in which delegates from all the federated states took part. The art of Phidias managed to prevent the richness of the materials used from lessening the dignity of the goddess. On the contrary it enhanced it. This statue was not, however, the final representation of the divinity in Greek art. In the second classical period, that of the fourth century, of which we possess one orginal masterpiece, the Hermes of Praxiteles, the divinity was shown turned completely from the exterior world, careless of its homage and absolutely absorbed in itself. This corresponds to Plato's idea of the godhead, which he conceived as perfect in itself and, therefore, self-sufficient.

When we go into the western part of the Parthenon we enter a different world. Here was a high and relatively narrow room whose ceiling was supported by four pillars or Ionic columns. It was used as a storehouse for the federal treasure and for the more precious of the votive offerings, which were also housed in the prodomus and in the principal cella. The opisthodomus, which did not communicate with the cella, but was shut off by gratings between the columns, served for the administration of the treasure. In antiquity a visitor to the Acropolis would find it easier than we do to realise that the western part formed the back of the temple. He left it on one side, and followed the Sacred Way, lined by innumerable votive offerings, finally arriving by way of the north colonnade to the front of the building.

The unusual arrangement of the interior was not visible from the exterior. The cella of a Greek temple is built on the plan of the primitive North European dwelling-house – a single room with a vestibule in front. The cella was designed at the same time as the sacred statue and was intended solely for its reception. There was no need to increase the inside space, for all ceremonial took place out of doors, in front of the altar placed in the sacred precinct. The addition of a peristyle and of the sloping roof and pediments, which joined it to the main building, was not due to the evolution of the interior distribution, but to the desire of altering the exterior appearance. A Greek sanctuary was essentially a sacred enclosure of which the temple occupied only a part. Whereas in the Middle Ages ordinary life went on round the cathedrals, and one only stepped on holy ground when one entered the porch, the Greek temple and its statue are placed in the centre of a sacred precinct which is separated from the outside world by high walls. Therefore Greek art could give its whole mind to the perfecting of the actual building to which the inner space was subordinated. It needed the genius of Ictinus to adapt the interior of the Parthenon to its dual employment, and yet make of the cella a room which fulfilled its traditional destiny in housing the sacred image.

Independence is as much a part of the nature of a Greek temple as of the statue which it contains. It has no artistic connection with anything exterior. It is not planned in relation to any other building near by, no symmetrical space surrounds it, and its marble steps rise straight up from the bare rock foundation on which it is built. The necessity for considering the surrounding space would have seemed to the Greek mind of those times a curtailment of liberty, a restriction of the independence of the building. In the same way a statue was not considered to have any connection either artistic or decorative with what surrounded it, for that might impair its dignity and effect. This belief in the absolute completeness of a work of art is an essential characteristic of the Greek spirit. We can understand it more easy as a philosophical theory, for we are so accustomed to grouping objects together that we have lost the power to isolate them. If a modern man could walk on the Acropolis of classical times, he would find himself sadly troubled by the amazing disorder which reigned there. Now that only four great classical buildings stand there, it is easier for us to understand and admire the perfect unity of the Parthenon.

Like all Greek temples, the Parthenon is built entirely of freestone blocks. Except for the bronze casings, which were fixed into the stone, and the wood of the casket ceiling and roof-frame, the only material used is marble. No mortar is used, and no rubble to fill gaps. No stone has an unexpected and unusual shape accidentally received in course of construction, as is the case in many mediaeval buildings, even the best constructed. The whole building is a symphony, in which each note, exactly calculated beforehand, adds to the harmony of the whole. It is, therefore, possible to replace the fallen stones in their original places. The technical execution of this building is possibly the finest that has ever been achieved on any building in the world. The blocks of marble join so perfectly that it is impossible to get even a knife-blade between them. The hand caresses with pleasure the roundness of the flutings and the smoothness even of the joints of drums and of capitals. Here is the perfection of building in this particular style, which still has power to amaze and astonish us, though modern architecture, working with other materials and faced with other tasks, has evolved different styles.

The beauties of this architecture consist in the exact proportions of the length, height and width, the static poise of the building, and the subordination of each part to the whole. The archaic temples of the sixth and even of the fifth centuries, with their narrow cellas and fronts, and long side colonnades, were weighed down by a heavy superstructure which was supported by massive columns often only one or two steps above the level of the ground. Each part sought to attract the visitor, without reference to the unity of the whole. An oppressive gravity hung about these buildings, which seemed ready to sink into the ground from their own weight. In the East, the Ionic temples were more gay and graceful. The columns were slimmer and delicately ornamented. Yet even they at times inclined in the archaic epoch to a certain ponderousness and disunity. In the Parthenon the superstructure is lighter, the column more slender. Both the Doric and the Ionic orders sought to discover the principles of harmony. In the Parthenon the heavy Doric architecture was supported by Ionic elements. But it is not only the proportions which have changed; the curves also have altered and become more sweeping. The entasis, or gentle swelling of the shaft, which in archaic columns seemed produced by the weight they supported, has now become a delicately organic movement, and the echinus of the capital, which was round and heavy, seems now to tend upwards towards the burden it must carry. The relations between the different parts of the column are also altered. Whereas previously the shaft and the echinus had each a separate existence, and the coping weighed heavily upon them, now these three parts form only one organism, which rises in a continuous line from the stylobate to the entablature. At the same time the line of the shaft and capital, and especially the curve of the echinus, give one the impression that the utmost limit of tension has been reached. Any difference in the proportions would destroy all appearance of stability, and a curve even slightly less rounded would break the flight of the column. The development of Doric architecture is not like a curved line, which mounts and then descends, but rather like the tension of a bowstring. The limit of this tension has been reached in the Parthenon. The slightest increase in the pull would snap it. As a matter of fact, the Parthenon was the culminating point of Doric evolution and its last manifestation. All later buildings are only feeble imitations. Doric architecture gives place to Ionic and later to the Corinthian style.

The Greek temple has no towers which aspire to heaven, but remains, solid and enduring, close to the earth. Yet its repose has no rigidity. To the balance between the pressure from above and the support from below were added refinements of technique which seem almost miraculous, to such a point that their very existence has been denied in some quarters. The walls of the cella are slightly inclined

33

towards the interior. All the columns follow this movement, the corner columns in the direction of the diagonal, and the antae in that of the columns which correspond to them. The axis of the column deviates from the perpendicular by 3 ins., the entasis is $^{7}/_{10}$ of an inch in a height of over 34 feet. The horizontal surface of the stylobate on which the columns stand has a convex curve, which is repeated in the architrave. The necessary corrections in the columns were made at the junctions of the lower and upper drums, and carried on through the entablature. The most astonishing thing is the curve of horizontal lines, which can be ascertained with certainty here as *14* in a few other Doric temples. The steps on which the building stands are not in a straight line, but have a convex curve, which on the back and front is of about $2^{1}/_{2}$ inches in 100 ft., and on the sides 4 inches in 215 ft. Recent measurements have proved that the columns on the north are all exactly 34 ft. 2.76 inches high, therefore the curve of the architrave is necessarily the same. Since all the joints are rigorously perpendicular, it is obvious that the front side of all the blocks of the stylobate and the architrave has the form of a parallelogram, which can only be measured with the most delicate instruments. A minute study of exact measures and calculations can alone make clear to us the amount of thought and precision which were given to the shaping of the marble. And not only these calculations but the organisation of the actual construction were done by a master mind and carried out by a strong personality.

Great pediments crowned majestically the back and front of the temple. Above them on the summit and at the ends were acroteria, formed of acanthus leaves and palmettes, graceful ornaments whose bright colours made them stand out clearly against the blue sky. Colour was used as a necessary element in the decoration of the building. All the ornamentation was coloured, the bands of the capital, the foliage and all the sculpture except the naked bodies. This use of colour heightened the effect of the metopes and triglyphs; the triglyphs were painted blue and the background of the metopes red. It was not just a faint wash but a thick layer of bright colours. To-day it has disappeared, but the action of weather and atmosphere, together with the bright light and the fine grain of the stone, has given the marble a golden brown tinge which has been compared to the colour of ripening corn.

For the sculptural adornment of the temple Phidias conceived a project far more ambitious than had ever yet been attempted for any building. Though he was not constrained by any fixed rules, he followed the traditional forms of monumental art, and the pediments were devoted to the goddess of the temple; on the east pediment was represented the birth of Athena, on the west her contest with Poseidon for the sovereignty of Attica. The metopes on the east showed the battles of gods and giants, while the other series were devoted to the struggles of the heroes: on the sides were the destruction of Ilium and the combat of the Lapiths and Centaurs, and below the west pediment the battle of the Athenians and the Amazons.

The idea of a frieze, which for the first time ornamented the cella of a Doric temple, was quite new. On this frieze the citizens of Athens advanced in a continuous procession towards the east, where an assembly of gods awaited them, Athena and Zeus in the middle. So the whole east front was the domain of the gods; as for the rest, the frieze was devoted to mortals, the metopes to heroes and the pediments to the gods. The different conditions of architectural surrounding necessitated a variation in the height and size of the reliefs. The instinctive feeling of te Greeks for a relation between subject and dimension brought about a natural gradation. The narrow frieze which ran like a ribbon round the wall of the cella showed in low relief the procession of the Panathenaea, and effaced itself with becoming modesty before the traditional decoration of the façade. In high relief, to suit the massive architectural frame in which they were set, stood out the heroic figures of the metopes, and finally on the pediments were placed the powerful and enormous statues of the gods.

A number of sculptors, chosen and instructed by Phidias, worked together at the execution of his projects. The building was finished in ten years; the metopes and the frieze must have been put into position before the colonnade was covered in or the roof begun, that is, probably, at the end of seven or eight years. The metopes were done first. They are still in place on the east, the west and above the north colonnade, but they have suffered so much damage that, though it is still possible to make out their subjects, we can no longer enjoy the detail of the figures. The metopes from the south side are nearly all in London, well preserved. We can study here the perfection of form and the harmony of the composition, but in the heavy northern air they lose all feeling of life and vigour. There is, however, one very fine one still in place on the south which, bathed in sunshine, helps us to realise the strength and beauty of these figures.

The metopes and triglyphs bound together as with a strong chain the upper part of the building, and alternated their different shapes and colours. Each metope formed a single slab which was slipped into the grooves of the triglyph blocks; it served no constructive purpose, and was merely a framed surface set on the face of the wall. At the same time it was not only ornamental. It was more a piece of decorative art where the subordination to the whole did not interfere with the completeness of each part. This can be found only in one other place – in Raphael's Vatican paintings.

The metopes of the Parthenon offer an enthralling spectacle. We can trace, from block to block, the way in which the art of composition, parallel with the development of the idea and the execution, rises to its highest point. Some of the sculpture, done by the older men, is angular and hesitating, as if the movement of the figures were paralysed by the small surface which contains them. Perfection

35

is reached in the blocks on the south, where each metope is absolutely self-contained, without reference to those on either side. The struggle between the man and the centaur is not only balanced, *18, 20* but fills the whole space, and, far from being constrained by the frame, develops freely inside it. The slightest tendency to carry the composition on, past the frame of the metope, would have upset the stability of the triglyphs and ruined the harmony of the alternation. Decorative sculpture in antiquity united freedom with subordination to the limits imposed. A different mentality is revealed by the sculpture of the Middle Ages, where the figures over the cathedral porches are cramped and crowded so as to follow the rhythm of the architecture.

The various themes represented by the metopes did not permit of them being all self-sufficient. It was necessary that those showing the destruction of Troy should be connected by some common bond, and in the combats of the Amazons and in those of the Giants some dominating figures accentuate the movement in one direction or another. But not all the metopes along one wall are connected. Some pieces form a group among themselves, and the end subjects are carefully chosen in order that no brusque movement shall destroy the sense of finality. It is impossible to detail the plan *19* followed, for it all depends on a certain sureness of feeling for form and rhythm which determines the place of each piece.

The workshop, under the direction of Phidias, had no resemblance to a modern workshop. Phidias worked at the gold and ivory statue of the Parthenos, and did not himself do the bas-reliefs, or even make models for them which could afterwards have been mechanically reproduced in marble. It was more than likely that he planned out the whole series and perhaps roughed out a few of the designs, but the actual execution was entrusted to a group of sculptors working under his orders. Therefore, each man had a great deal of liberty, and so each piece has, besides the inspiration of a master mind, an attractive touch of originality. When work was begun, a great many different tendencies and schools were grouped together. Phidias had to choose and train his collaborators in the course of the work.

His strong will had already imposed a certain uniformity on his helpers when the frieze of the cella was begun. Up till now no Doric temple had had its cella decorated in this way. The Ionic friezes were smaller and did not run round all four sides. For the first time contemporary figures and events, though deprived of any personal application, were used in the decoration of a temple. Phidias did not choose for his innovation the front of the building, but made of it a band of sculpture which crowned the outer wall of the cella and which was a little narrower than the slabs of the metopes. The subject of it was the procession of the Panathenaea which travelled slowly towards the gods waiting on the east front. In this way the frieze became a great commemorative picture. The

36

artistic and religious sentiment of the time caused the frieze to be executed down to the last detail with precision and care, though no one could get near enough to it to look closely at the finish of the various parts. The figures on the frieze were not planned in any relation to the spectator, nor even to the place which they were to occupy under the ceiling, where only a faint and indirect light showed up their multicoloured relief. We can now stand directly in front of the slabs, which are out in the full light of day, and see them as they appeared at their completion to the men who worked on them.

The Panathenaea, consecrated to the goddess of the city, were the final and crowning point of the national festival of Attica. Not only the citizens took part in them, but also any strangers who were at Athens, and delegates from all the federated states. Every four years, on the morning of the last day of the festival, the peplos woven for the old statue of Athena Polias was carried in solemn procession to the citadel. The sports and musical competitions had taken place the day before, and the victors marched in the procession or took their place in the line of chariots and horses. Phidias did not try to represent the procession of any one year, which would have seemed to the Greeks a transitory thing, quite unworthy of a place on the walls of a temple, and not even worthy to figure as the subject of an artistic composition. It was more the idea of the procession that he attempted to portray, divorced from any temporal or individual sense. The political importance of the building was stressed by this commemorative picture. The idea of democracy which one has described as the political form of humanity found here in its classic form has been portrayed pictorially in this frieze. The frieze contains no portraits, but only types. It is characteristic of the nature of Greek art that these figures are not only free from any personal traits, but also from any individual element, which a sculptor of the Renaissance could not have resisted giving even to abstract figures. The sublimity of the Greek conception of art lies in the fact that it portrayed the human body as an abstraction of beauty, without any individual characteristics. This abstract conception of the human figure causes a certain surprise which our historic sense must overcome, for on the other hand the eternal validity and completeness of the Greek ideal of beauty transcends all boundaries of time and people.

The frieze represents a continuous procession whose movement is in itself and does not disturb the static character of the temple. At the same time, its relation with the building, which would be lacking if it surrounded the cella wall without a break, advancing always in the same sense, is preserved by the ingenious device of dividing it in two, and bringing it up each side to the east 48, 49 front, where the gods and heroes of the tribes are waiting to receive it. The group of gods surrounding Athena and Zeus is also divided in two, and each section turns to face the procession advancing on each side. In the centre of the two groups of gods one can see the priests bearing the peplos.

They have already reached the sanctuary. In this way the procession is arranged in relation to the east front, and conforms thus to the architectural design of the whole building. In order to prevent the people in the procession turning their backs on each other on the west front, which would have been absurd, Phidias made the break at the south-west corner, and slowed down the whole movement along this west side, which is incorporated with the north side, by showing the Athenian knights still busy with their preparations, some not even mounted, while others are just moving into position. This arrangement has also the advantage that anyone entering the temple after coming along the Sacred Way, and seeing first the frieze on the west side, could then follow it along the north, and see it as a whole from its departure to its arrival in front of the solemn assembly of gods.

The frieze has suffered in many ways and at many hands. It may indeed be said to have had a tragic destiny. While to-day its slabs are among the most precious treasures of European art, the Greeks and Romans, with their wealth of sculptural masterpieces, seem to have neglected them. The frieze was never described or copied during antiquity. It was first brought into prominence when Lord Elgin took the greater part of it to London. Some of the slabs are in the Acropolis Museum, one of the most beautiful in the Louvre. Only on the west we admire a continuous run of slabs, *47, 22-41* which are mostly in position. Two slabs on the south side can also be seen, but they are in a most *38* battered condition. They all can only be seen from a distance, and recent photographs have shown how rapidly they are deteriorating. When we compare them with a cast taken some time ago, we can *39, 40* see how much we have already lost. *Pl. 17, 18*

And yet it is in these very pieces that the frieze becomes a reality to us. It is exactly proportioned to the whole architectural structure. The figures are set on a band which is ornamented with Doric facets. It is edged by a beautiful line of Ionic foliage, which was formed of red and white leaves on a blue background, leading up to a scroll which in turn was surmounted by Doric foliage. Though the colours of the frieze have disappeared, the detail of form is even more clearly visible in the clear outdoor light. It is astonishing that this excess of light, which was never intended to reach the frieze, does not spoil the effect of the sculpture, but, on the contrary, gives it an added beauty. We must con- *27, 32, 33* clude that the figures were not planned with particular reference to the indirect light which they were destined to receive, but with a feeling for the relief usual on such decorations, which in most cases stood out of doors. The bas-reliefs were not done on the walls of the building, after the slabs had been put in position, but on the ground, either in the open air or in a well lighted workshop. One can gather this from the fact that the feet of the figures throughout the frieze do not touch the bottom of the slab, but are cut away from the edge so that they should not be damaged when the slab was slipped into place.

All that remains on the Parthenon of this great work of art is a triumphant glorification of the Attic cavalry. Phidias has represented wonderfully in this procession the modesty of the young girls, the pride of the young men and the dignity of the elders. But he has surpassed all this, and employed his genius to the full, in this long line of youthful horsemen. Phidias, an Athenian by birth, spoke in this to the heart of the people of Attica, who always admired above all things the beauty of a horse and the art of horsemanship. The writers of classical tragedy spoke with enthusiasm of this country of wonderful horses and superb riders. The writings of Xenophon on horsemanship and the handling of cavalry bear witness to a consummate skill and knowledge in everything pertaining to the horse. "If a man wishes to own a horse which can be used in solemn procession, which will stand out for its distinction and bearing, let him remember that these qualities cannot be found in every horse; the one he chooses must have a noble spirit and a strong and vigorous body." Later he describes the perfect horse: "An animal at once noble, docile, proud, strong, pleasing to the eye, and yet terrifying." This is the state of mind which was responsible for the beautiful horses on the frieze of the Parthenon. Goethe found in the horse's head from
56 the east pediment the ideal horse. He calls it the prototype "Urpferd", and since his time the beauty of the horses on the Parthenon has always been celebrated. Victor Cherbuliez expresses this admira-
30, 36 tion in his "Un cheval de Phidias" ending a hymn to one of the horses on the west frieze with these words: "Tu es la force qui se connaît et se possède, tu es la beauté qui jouit d'elle-même, tu es ce qu'il y a de meilleur et de plus précieux dans l'humanité."

The horseman united two objects particularly venerated by the Greeks, youth and horse, in the wonderful unity which real horsemanship creates between a horse and his rider. The technique of riding was different then from what it is to-day. The Athenian mounted bare-legged without saddle or stirrups, and used a bridle, but no bit. The horses were smaller than those we know, though probably not quite as small as they are represented on the frieze, where it was necessary to diminish them a little in order to be able to bring together in one frame horsemen and pedestrians.

Eight slabs of the west frieze, forming an uninterrupted sequence, are so well preserved that photographs of them can render the beauties and the harmony of composition and details without any need of a commentary. They speak so clearly that amplification and interpretation are alike useless. Each of these pieces can be isolated and regarded separately. This is not true of the slabs
46 on the sides. If we look at those in the Acropolis Museum, the elders chosen for their manly bearing,
45, 44 the young men carrying on their shoulders heavy vases, or a single detail of the line of sacrificial animals, we realise that the composition has ceased to regard the joint of the slab, and goes beyond it. It is a continuous procession which occupies the whole of the frieze. On the east again,

as on the west, each piece is complete in itself. One of them, now in the Louvre, contains the head *47*
of the procession with a group of girls walking in couples. On another slab we see a group formed *48*
by Poseidon, Apollo, and Artemis. Consideration of the decorative problem was again the cause of
this variance. On the sides it was possible for the continuity to be uninterrupted. The front needed
a calmer composition, in which each part should be perfectly harmonised. And even this harmony
needed to be different at each end. The same feeling caused the frieze on the fronts to be more closely
connected with the architectural design of the building by the use of facets, a motif which was
borrowed from the triglyphs.

A great number of people worked at the frieze. Some were still under the influence of archaic
art, others have never been surpassed in technique. Softly rounded limbs neighbour with dry
angular lines, bold execution with weak. There is an amazing difference between the heads of the
figures on the west, and again between those on the north. The personal character of each different
piece of work exercises an irresistible fascination. This combination of two talents, that of the
master who designs, and that of the pupil who executes, is common in antiquity. These personal
differences are delightful nevertheless. The overpowering impression is that of the almost unima-
ginable unity of the whole. It was designed entirely by Phidias, and finished in a few years. Those
who worked for him had in front of them a design which fixed the composition and subject of
each slab. The master was always present to watch, and if necessary correct, their interpretation
of his plan. From the fact that he was able to bend so many workers to his will and so impregnate
them with his style we can judge of the extent of his genius and of his dominating personality.

Phidias was already an old man when he finished the statue of the Parthenos. His last task was
to finish off the great building he had begun by the sculptures of the pediments. They have been
so damaged that we can no longer judge of their general effect, though we can still admire the
artistry of each separate piece. On the west pediment were statues of the legendary king Cecrops *54, 10*
and of his daughter who presses close to him, awed by the scene she is called upon to witness.
These figures have been eaten away by wind and rain through thousands of years. Where once the
drapery flowed in graceful folds over their rounded limbs is nothing but a confused and jagged
edge of stone, which seems on the point of crumbling to dust. Not far from this group, in the left
angle of the pediment, was a statue of the river-god Cephisus, which, together with the greater
part of the other remains, is to-day one of the most precious treasures of the British Museum. There
we can still admire the astonishing perfection of the limbs, strong and yet gracefully languid as
if in the water. Very little remains of the central statues, Athena and Poseidon, whose powerful
figures faced one another in the centre of the pediment, too little for us to be able to reconstruct

40

them. Here, as in the east pediment, which represented the birth of Athena, the central and culminating point of divine action is lost. We can only follow its effect on the figures ranged on each side, figures divine or legendary, witnesses of these events, until all excitement is lost in the calm and eternal steadiness of the natural powers represented in the angles. In the left angle of the

12 east pediment one can still see traces of the heads of the horses who formed the second pair of the

56 sun-god's chariot. The front pair are in London, with the head of the horse attached to the chariot of

55 the moon-goddess, plunging beneath the waves. On one side was a group of three women who served as intermediaries between the elemental spirits of the sun and moon and the divine beings in the centre. In the marvellous flow and sweep of their draperies one can recognise the characteristic traits of Phidias's later style. We cannot be certain that he sculptured them himself, but his influence is apparent in every one of them. They were probably entrusted to the best sculptors of all those had assisted in the execution of the frieze and the metopes. The individuality which can be found in every piece of sculpture on the Parthenon is easily distinguishable here. But these slight variations in the manner of treating bodies and draperies do not impair the unity of the inspiration which is responsible for both pediments. An imposing subject, imposing forms and an imposing artistic conception here go hand in hand. This classical art needed to do nature no violence in order to obtain its effect. Its perfection is absolutely natural. Immediately after the completion of the Parthenon Athens was plunged into the disastrous Peloponnesian war. No one dared attack Pericles himself, but they touched him through the artist who was dear to him. Phidias was accused of stealing the gold and ivory which had been allotted for the statue of the Parthenos, and died in prison.

As soon as the Parthenon was finished, the great army of experienced sculptors and stone-masons who had worked at it found themselves confronted with another great task, the building of the Propylaea. The chief architect of the Parthenon having had to go to Eleusis in connection with some other work, the planning of the Propylaea was entrusted to another not otherwise known to us, named Mnesicles. The same material was used as for the Parthenon, the same skilled technique, and enormous sums of money were voted for this building which was to be in no way unworthy of the great temple. When the Parthenon was begun, it was most probably intended to make the Acropolis one vast sanctuary, with a great entrance gate, and perhaps to replace the early temple. It was not intended to weld all the different buildings into a composite whole, which would have been contrary to the spirit of the time, but to organise the work in such a way as to render its distribution more easy and so make it less of a burden. All other building was stopped and everybody was set to work on the Parthenon, thus making certain that it would be finished to time. In 438 work began on the Propylaea with the same speed, but was interrupted by the outbreak of the Peloponnesian war.

The Propylaea are: "a step, a door, an entrance, a vestibule, a space between the interior and the exterior, between the sacred and the profane" (Goethe: *Einleitung in die Propyläen.*) In religious architecture in Greece this idea of a door isolated with its vestibule derives from the conception of a sanctuary as a sacred precinct. It was, and still is, usual in Greece to cover wooden doors with a penthouse as a protection against bad weather. In this way one had already a form of door before temples were thought of, and during the whole of antiquity there existed precincts consecrated to a divinity, which had a propylon but no temple. In the vestibule the worshipper had time to compose himself before crossing the threshold of the sanctuary. The porch of the mediaeval cathedral served the same purpose. It was a part of the sanctuary which yet had nothing to do with the actual sacred precinct. At the western end of the hill in Mycenaean times was the main entrance to the royal castle. During the centuries when the Acropolis formed a town, properly speaking, it was retained as a fortified door. Each little sanctuary, and particularly the precinct containing the sacred tree and spring, had probably its own propylon. The sons of Peisistratus raised a great marble door of which the greater part was incorporated into later buildings, but of which one corner is still standing on the furthest south-east side. This door was still to be seen rising up, narrow and cramped, between fragments of the old cyclopean wall. Mnesicles was given the task of raising a building which would be an entrance worthy of a sanctuary which should include the whole of the Acropolis. He joined the actual entrance to side buildings which crowned the west front of the rock with a magnificent piece of architecture. By the use of the plural instead of the singular, the word that Herodotus had used to designate the vestibules of Egyptian temples, the significance of the building was made clear. It was to be a door and a vestibule to a sanctuary; from now onwards the Acropolis was to be given over entirely to religious services, though in time of need it could be temporarily fortified and used as a refuge.

The central point of the building is the entrance, which is absolutely independent. There were five doors, the largest in the middle, those on each side smaller and narrower. The centre door corresponded to a central aisle in the main hall, the smaller ones to two smaller aisles intended *1* for pedestrians. Thus the idea of a wall is preserved in the construction of a piece of monumental architecture which makes its effect even when seen from a distance. It has been copied in the Propylaea at Munich. On each side was a vestibule bounded by side walls and opening on to a colonnade. Each of these colonnades had a sloping roof, like a temple, but, owing to the irregularity of the ground, that on the outside was lower than that on the inside.

The architect has very cleverly made use of the rising ground in planning his building. The road wound up precipitously to the front of the Propylaea. To-day the effect is a little falsified on the *58* right because of the marble slabs that the baroque sentiment of the time of the Roman empire placed in front of the Propylaea, uniting rock and building in a way which certainly did not lack majesty. But to the Greek it was natural that there should be no transition from the rough ground of the path to the clean lines of the building. Four steps led to a portico, as in a temple. Under the central intercolumniation the steps were interrupted, in order that the road followed by horsemen and by sacrificial animals, and taken also by the procession of the Panathenaea, might rise *61–63* in a gentler slope. The pedestrian entered on the left and right by a much longer portico. Two rows of three columns each, which stood on the edge of the Sacred Way, carried the roof and divided the room. The front of the building was designed after the Doric order, but Mnesicles made the inside columns Ionic. He may not have been the first to think of employing in one building, in order to obtain two separate effects, these two styles, which came from different countries and were the products of different races, but this is the first time we find the idea put into practice. The severe majesty of the Doric order was reserved for the façade, the grace and lightness of the Ionic for the interior. The spectator is conscious of the contrast between the simple but imposing structure of the Doric column and the elegance with which the slender and less deeply grooved Ionic shaft rises from its base towards the rich decoration of its capital. This contrast can be felt everywhere, in front of the doors, in the portico or when one turns back to look through the doors. One column has been put back into place and once again supports a part of the casket ceiling, limiting the height of the *62, 64, 68* room. Here between the walls, the columns, the pavement, and the ceiling of marble, one feels even more keenly the enchantment which flows from the beauty of this building.

Through the doors one could see right across the Attic plain. Four steps further on and one *62, 63* stood in front of the west front of the Parthenon. Then one came upon other buildings, and on *65, 11* the enormous number of votive offerings which strewed the ground, and which were hidden by high walls from the outer world. Through the narrower inside portico one came out on the citadel. This second portico was only raised on one step, unlike the temples, which usually had several.

Old photographs show us the state of the inside portico before the work of reconstruction was undertaken. The drums of the columns were displaced by an earthquake; only a few isolated columns are joined here and there by the remains of the entablature. The broken remnants of the superstructure lie scattered on the ground. The ruins rise dark against the clear sky, and beside them stands the Frankish tower, black and threatening. A picturesque sight, but in nothing has it the sentiment of antiquity. To-day the columns rise once more in the beauty of their tension and rounded curves, carrying the marvellously adapted weight of the entablature. It has even been found possible to replace a part of the pediment. A recent photograph shows us the marble splendour *59* of this reconstructed building, but there are black shadows between the columns which by contrast make them and the entablature appear suddenly flat; at the same time the oblique view seems to bring in question the stability of the edifice. The men of classical times must have regarded these buildings from various positions. But the beauty of a Greek façade is only fully to be realised when one stands directly in front of it, and the relief of its forms does not appear with absolute clarity unless the eye can follow them into the warm transparent shadows without being troubled by a sudden blinding contrast.

The plan of Mnesicles went beyond a mere entrance. Other buildings were to join on to it, without harming its independence and its central position. Symmetrically on each side and a little way back he planned to build two wide porticoes opening by a colonnade in antae towards the Acropolis. To their back walls would have been joined two smaller buildings opening on the

44

west towards the exterior, with their inner sides, which would have flanked the western front of the Propylaea, facing the ascent. The west front of the south building was planned as a colonnade and to be used as a through-passage to the temple of Athena Nike, whilst the west front oft the north building, which was raised on a high foundation wall, was necessarily a wall, there being no room for a terrace. Two lateral antae and a frieze of triglyphs would have given the illusion of a façade. The sloping roof of these two buildings would also have been turned towards the west. The sides which followed the rise of the ground were to have had a front row of columns which would have had to be asymmetric, in order to allow one of them to be in line with the front of the Propylaea. This grandiose plan allowed for several different buildings, and sacrificed the interior symmetry of the two wings; it made of the Propylaea a façade for the western end of the citadel, a building for the reception of those coming from the town, and an edifice turned towards the sanctuary. Mnesicles, in the extent of his architectural conceptions, was far in advance of his time and was not allowed to execute his project. We do not know what these various buildings were destined to contain. It is certain that they would have had nothing to do with the actual ceremonies, which took place within the sanctuary. This is obvious from their shape. The great interior porticoes might perhaps, like those of a market hall, have been used for the administration of the Acropolis, and at the same time served to shelter visitors from sun and rain. The smaller buildings could also have been used for some such purpose. All would probably have been decorated with painting.

Only a part of the original plan was used. From the very beginning it met with opposition. Already when laying the foundations it was found necessary to give up the plan of the east porticoes and to reduce the south-west colonnade to a narrow passage. We should know nothing of the original plan if Mnesicles, considering its curtailment only a temporary measure, had not so arranged matters that it could easily be returned to later on. For this reason we find beside the west portico antae inclined in the sense of the projected row of columns. It is probable that the architect and the commission appointed to oversee the building of the Propylaea met with some opposition which they hoped later to overcome. We can even suppose that the opposition came from the administrators and protectors of the existing temples, which would have suffered from the execution of the plan in its original form. The two south porticoes would have encroached on the precincts of Artemis Brauronia and of Athena Nike. The remains of the old walls of the citadel would have had to be pulled down. Consequently a struggle arose between those who wished to make the Acropolis an official sanctuary for the State religion, to which all the different cults would have had to submit, and those who remained obstinately faithful to the old tradition.

Different political factions may also have turned this dissension to their own ends. We have seen that Pericles, who was the driving force, if not the actual master, behind the building of the Parthenon, as well as of the Propylaea, could not do as he wished in 438, and was obliged to be satisfied with a compromise. His hope, and that of his architect, of getting his own way eventually was finally shattered by the outbreak of the Peloponnesian war in 431. The edifice was finished, with the curtailment imposed by the oppositon, but the finishing touches had not been given to the walls. On the outside of the building chisel marks can clearly be seen on the rough surface of the stone, and the projections left to help the masons to get the blocks into position are still *66* there. The blocks were not given a smooth finish until they were in place. The projections and a rough projecting panel, which should have been chipped away, can still be seen on the lower edge and sides of the antae. Even the inside walls, which appear so perfect, were not completely finished. The joints are still surrounded by a slight margin, which was intended to prevent the *62* edge of the block from being damaged when it was placed on another. Afterwards this extra width was taken away, and the joint was practically imperceptible. The slabs of the pavement, too, were never perfectly finished, and the building remained as it had been left at the beginning of the Peloponnesian war. If the Propylaea lack the finished perfection of the Parthenon, they yet afford us an opportunity of following the development of this most beautiful building, and later generations have found beauty even in this incompleteness, and have intentionally made use of it for the sake of its artistic effect.

46

TEMPLE OF ATHENA NIKE

South-west of the Propylaea the rock rises in a narrow ledge, reinforced by a bastion. This 70 strip of ground was outside the sacred precinct, and on it was built a small temple, from which one could look across to the sea, and from which, according to an old legend, Egeus threw himself when he saw Theseus's ship returning from Crete with black sails. This place, guarding the entrance to the Acropolis, was the site of a small precinct from very early times, with an altar dedicated to the warrior maiden regarded as the goddes of victory, Athena Nike.

A decree of the people in 448 ordered that a priestess of Athena Nike should be appointed, and that a gate, a temple and an altar designed by Callicrates should be built. New foundation walls were raised in order to enlarge the site, and the little temple was begun. But hardly were the first stones in position before the work was stopped. This was probably due to the influence of Pericles and Phidias, who were anxious to prevent any new building rising haphazard. They had already in mind the plan of the Propylaea, and did not want to be hindered in the execution of this great architectural project by buildings previously raised without reference to it. When, however, the building of the Propylaea was actually started the opposition was strong enough to insist on the curtailment of the original plan, though it could not succeed in getting the little Temple of Athena Nike finished. This was only done after the Peace of Nicias in 421, when there was a respite in the tragic struggle between Athens and Sparta. The final touches were not given until 405.

Like some rare jewel this slim marble edifice rises, white and gleaming, above the sombre rock foundation. Though small, the site gives the first essential of a Greek temple, absolute freedom and independence. The west front is built right on the edge of the rock. Consequently there is an open space before the east front separating the building from the Propylaea overlooking it, and per- mitting an uninterrupted view of the edifice. Anyone climbing up towards the Acropolis could 70, 71 easily distinguish the details of its construction. It rises on three levels on the principle of an amphiprostyle, and has a portico of four Ionic columns back and front of the cella. The little 72 sanctuary had no vestibule, but was open to the east along its whole length. The space between two inside pillars served as an entrance, while the sides were closed by iron gratings. At the back of the cella wall were two antae, thus preserving the exterior symmetry. In the cella stood a wooden statue of the goddess, holding in her right hand a pomegranate and in her left a helmet. When, later on, people wondered at this statue, so different from the usual conception of the Nike, the legend grew up that the goddess of victory had been represented wingless, in order that she should be forced to remain at Athens.

The Ionic order was chosen for this little temple, for though the great main temple could only be built in the traditional Doric style, for this small sanctuary the graceful Ionic form was thought more suitable. Above the columns formed of the usual three parts – base, shaft, and capital – is placed an entablature divided into three bands. Above this is a frieze running round all four sides, *74, 75* with small figures standing out in bold relief in the strong sunlight. Since the restoration of the temple was completed in 1940, the frieze is covered by the entablature again, and one can very *72* well imagine the gable-roof sloping to the ridge.

If one compares the columns of the Nike temple with those of the Propylaea or the Erechtheum, one notices immediately that they produce a more archaic impression. They are shorter and more sturdy, and the base is not yet made in the Attic style in use since the time of the Propylaea, consisting of an upper and lower torus separated by a deeply curved groove. But above all they have none of the classic harmony of line, and the three sections of the column do not seem to have been made in proportion. The transition from the base to the shaft is too abrupt, and the capitals are relatively too heavy. In these columns one can detect something of that angularity and groping technique which characterises the transition period from archaic to classical art. But the figures of the east frieze are very like the caryatides of the Erechtheum which date from about 420. This apparent incongruity is explained when we consider the history of the building. When it was first begun the bases, the shafts and probably the capitals of the columns were executed from the designs of Callicrates, at a time when the sculptors of the Parthenon figures were fighting against the shackles of archaic art. These various parts remained scattered about when work was interrupted and were finally put together in 421. It is unlikely that designs which were by then so out of date were used, but the material ready to hand was utilised, and on it was placed an architrave and a frieze which conformed to contemporary artistic standards.

Four slabs of the frieze were taken to London by Lord Elgin. Their places are occupied by terra-cotta casts. Many others are missing, and nearly all have suffered great damage. On the north and south sides were represented combats between Greeks and Persians, on the west combats between Greeks and Greeks. These most certainly do not represent contemporary struggles, but

48

the already legendary battle of Plataea. The animation of the fight fills the frieze with a crowd of moving figures, and the detail of loose floating robes accentuates the feeling of tension. The artists who executed the frieze have brought into harmony the different groups of combatants and woven into a rhythmic pattern the contrasting movements. One slab which is relatively well preserved gives us an excellent idea of the detail. A Persian soldier is slipping from his wounded horse, which is about to crash on to the body of a man lying on the ground. A Greek soldier is seizing upon his enemy, about to deal him a mortal blow, while on the right a second Persian comes to the help of his comrade. The east side is quite different. It shows an assembly of gods grouped symmetrically about Athena. Some are seated, but most of them stand full face, in easy and graceful

74, 75   attitudes, their robes falling in long soft folds about them. In spite of the ravages of time, the splendour and vigour of these marble figures is most striking.

The sanctuary of Athena Nike received a new adornment when, after the last brilliant victories of the Athenians in 408, Alcibiades returned to the city in triumph. The edge of the bastion was surrounded by a parapet. On the outside, visible from far off, ran a frieze celebrating the victories of Athens. On each of the three sides – north, west and south – Athena, seated on a rock, watches

76   the winged Victories decking trophies, or bringing animals to sacrifice. One Nike is about to place

73   a helmet on a trophy, another is untying her sandal before crossing the threshold of the sanctuary,

77   two others are struggling with a recalcitrant bull. The spirit in which this frieze is conceived contrasts with the directness and simplicity of the Parthenon frieze. In the latter an overwhelming vitality has been schooled to the restraint of classical art, while here it is as if a virtuoso played an instrument left him by his master, drawing from the sweep of limbs and draperies new and more mannered harmonies. This balustrade is a hymn to victory, full of the passionate exultation of those last military successes, which came to the Athenians after so many years of distress and preceded their final downfall.

ERECHTHEUM

The Parthenon and the Propylaea were already finished, and still the richly-decorated wooden statue of Athena, which the Athenians had managed to convey on board one of their ships and so save from destruction at the hands of the Persians, stood in the ruins of the old temple, which, deprived of its peristyle and of its pediments, had been hastily set in order for the reception of the sacred image. Nothing was further from the thoughts of the Athenians at this time than to transfer the wooden statue to the Parthenon, which had not been built to replace the earlier building but as a second temple with its own statue. On the contrary, it was intended that this older statue, to which clung all the traditions of piety and ceremonial, should remain in the early temple close to the sacred objects which for perhaps some thousands of years had been associated with the cult of Athena; but it was soon seen that the wooden image could only temporarily be housed here, and it is probable that Pericles and Phidias had already thought of building a temple for Athena which should be worthy of her. However, the outbreak of the Peloponnesian war hindered the execution of this project.

The war, however, did not hinder the intellectual and artistic development of Athens, and during the years of the war of Archidamos, 431–421, immense progress was made. Soon after the beginning of hostilities, the history of Herodotus appeared, and Thucydides conceived the idea of chronicling the events of the war. Sophocles and Euripides were at the height of their fame, and political comedy was a rival of tragedy. The problems of philosophy and of human education were given a new and more profound basis in the teachings of Socrates and of the Sophists. There was a great deal of dissension and parties were formed which differed fundamentally not only on political matters but intellectually. In the midst of this great activity of mind and body, which was fostered by the rapidity of contemporary events, plastic arts suffered a certain neglect. Sculpture and painting found a field of activity, though a somewhat limited one, in the preparation of votive offerings, but no big enterprises were undertaken by the State, and all building was at a standstill. At the same time the need felt not only by individuals but by the people as a whole for self-expression in art is proved by the fact that, during the periods of tranquillity which followed the treaty of 421 and the victories of Alcibiades, advantage was taken of the lull for the carrying out of religious duties and the realisation of various projects in architecture and sculpture. In the first peaceful years the temple of Athena Nike was built and the building of the Erechtheum, whose principal cella was intended for the old wooden image, was considerably advanced. In the elation of later victories this building was quickly finished and the balustrade of the Nike temple put into position.

Pl. 1   The new building was in the immediate vicinity of the early temple of Athena. In this way the early centre of worship would be incorporated, while, at the same time, the new temple, by its distance from the Parthenon, retained its individuality. The wooden statue could remain on its original site during the actual building, which took longer than had originally ben intended. For, during the disastrous events of the war, its construction had to be suspended, though the walls were already up, the Caryatid portico finished and the columns of the east portico even fluted. But in 409 a commission reported on the state of the building and the material prepared for its continuation, and, during the next two years, it was finished. The accounts, which have for the most part been preserved, give us some idea of the time taken and of the nature of the construction. Under the Romans the building was damaged by fire, and subsequently restored, many pieces being replaced by copies.

The new building was far smaller than the early temple, and Ionic in style. Pericles had probably planned it so, for there was no reason to place another Doric edifice beside the Parthenon. The aesthetic contrast between the two buildings, which we so clearly realise to-day, was probably unnoticed by the people of that time. They only knew that it was necessary to erect a temple for the small archaic statue of Athena as well as for the Heroes and sacred objects worshipped in her precinct, and that the graceful Ionic style was more suitable for such a purpose than the Doric. The conception and execution of the building are typical of the generation of 421, quite different from that which erected the Parthenon. The Parthenon was sacred to the divinity of the State, and represents the whole nation at the very height of its political power; the Erechtheum, on the contrary, reflects the spirit of a party which combined an aristocratic conservatism with a sort of naive piety. They sought to endow the traditional objects and places of worship with the most exquisite work of art possible. The leader of this party was the general Nicias, who never made a decision without having recourse to prophecies and divine guidance, in contrast to Pericles, who was above all such superstition. The plan on which the Erechtheum was built was as far removed from the generally accepted rules of Greek architecture as were the Propylaea of Mnesicles, but for a very different reason. Mnesicles wished to subordinate the temples to a general unity and co-ordination of line; the architect of the Erechtheum endeavoured to provide for every necessity of the cult and ceremonial without reference to the unity of the building.

In spite of much research on the subject a great deal about this building, especially the plan of the interior and the significance of the various rooms, remains obscure. The position of the various sacred objects, as well as the conformation of the ground, played a large part in the planning of its unusual shape. The south and east sides were on considerably higher ground than the west and north sides. The main body of the temple, properly speaking, is planned in relation to the east *84, 85* front and the south side. It forms a cella on whose east side is a colonnade. It was impossible to make a corresponding colonnade on the west owing to the ground being so much lower. Never-theless the wall opened in a series of columns, and it was only in Roman times that the spaces *81, 86* between these were filled up as they are to-day. When the sloping roof was in position above the cella, the temple, seen from the heights of the citadel, looked quite normal. For the wall under the western colonnade, with its asymmetric door, was not visible from the summit of the Acropolis and was moreover hidden by an outside wall from anyone approaching from the north-west.

The interior of the cella was quite irregular. By the east portico one entered into a narrow room where stood, presumably, the statue of Athena Polias. The western part, which was divided into several rooms, was on a much lower level. Under the south-west corner was the site of the tomb of Cecrops, inside was the sacred salt spring, and in one of the rooms Erechtheus was worshipped. On the west a small door led into the sacred precinct of Pandrosos, daughter of Cecrops, where grew the sacred olive-tree of Athena. This was part of the original sacred precinct of Athena Polias, the primitive sanctuary of the citadel. A great staircase leading to these western rooms could only be built on the north wall. On this side of the building there was also a wide portico which ran *87, 90* out beyond the west wall of the building. Its shape is easily explained by the threefold use for which it was destined. It was not only a vestibule for the west cella, but a propylon for the precinct of Pandrosos and like a monopteron over the trident-marks of Poseidon. Over these marks in accordance with tradition an opening was created in the coffered ceiling and roof above it leaving it open to the sky. From the higher south terrace of the citadel, where the ruins of the early temple stood until 406, a staircase inside a small portico led down to the west side of the cella. Six statues *83* of young girls supported the entablature of this portico, which follows the line of the west side of *92, 93* the temple, and has no relation to the north portico.

The building, therefore, consists of three parts, which bear no relation to one another but are complete in themselves, and seem to have come together by chance. The picturesque unity which we see to-day was not discernible to a Greek eye. A mediaeval architect would have brought these various parts together by some common element of design; the Greek architect would not sacrifice the independence of the three parts. He who visited the temple in classical times was conscious of the religious unity of the whole, but enjoyed the architectural perfection of each section in the same way as in a group of statues he considered each one alone. We shall therefore do more justice to the building if we consider each part separately — the cella and the two side porticoes.

84 The effect of the east front is spoiled by the absence of the corner column, which has been taken to London. But the remaining columns rise before us in rhythmic harmony. The Ionic style knew nothing of curved horizontals. The columns have no entasis, but are constructed with a delicacy *88, 89* and judgement which speak of an amazing mastery of technique and are comparable only to the columns of the Parthenon in this respect. All the columns lean slightly towards the wall, deviating about one inch in a height of 20 ft. The corner columns are also inclined in the same degree towards the centre. The architect would probably not have taken the trouble to calculate such a small and subtle difference had he not been well aware what vitality and lightness were imparted to the building by these almost imperceptible differences. As Paul Valéry says in "Eupalinos" they are "des inflexions infimes et toutes puissantes".

The ornamentation of the columns and of the entablature is far richer than that of the Propylaea *102, 103* or the Temple of Athena Nike. Round the neck of the column is a band of palmette and flower pattern in relief, with egg and dart moulding above, and above that again a torus ornamented with a rich plait; the coussinets were heavily sculptured, and in the eye of the volutes on each side of the capital was a bronze rosette. Bright colours heightened the decorative effect of all this *99, 101* moulding. Round the wall of the cella ran a frieze surmounted by a band of palmette and flower pattern with an egg and dart moulding and a row of heart-shaped leaves. The leaves, which in the older edifices were usually painted on, are here executed in relief, as are those of the entablature and the cornice. The frieze was one of the most striking features of the building. The figures were not sculptured in the blocks of which it was formed, but were cut separately in white Pentelic marble and attached to a background of black Eleusinian stone. This technique, so contrary to the usages of Greek architecture and sculpture, is known to us by the figures on the bases of gold and ivory statues. We feel in the decoration of the frieze and the capitals, so unlike the simplicity of earlier buildings, a tendency towards decorative art. Yet nowhere is the decoration overdone nov disturbing the havmony of the whole; it is possible that its use is due to the fact that the builders of the Erechtheum looked on it as a necessary religious element. The figures on the frieze have many features in common with those on the balustrade of the Nike temple, but here the passion which is expressed there is softened.

The proportions of the different parts of the building were settled with absolute finality, but the stonemasons who cut the ornamentation from a model were allowed a certain margin for the expression of individuality, which gives all these decorative details an added interest. We realise the amount of work that was demanded by the lavish decoration of this temple when we consider that the fluting of one column alone – which was done in four phases, from the first smoothing of the stone to the final polish – occupied a group of five to seven workmen for about two months. This explains the perfect regularity which is nevertheless free from any mechanical uniformity.

The statues of young girls which support the entablature of the south portico, though also *94, 95* sculptured by different hands, have no disparity, and fit harmoniously into the whole. Here again we can admire the organisation of an Attic workshop, where one master hand directed everything, but where each worker was allowed to express himself within the limits of conformity. The movement of the bodies and the treatment of the draperies are quite different from those of the figures on the Parthenon frieze. The Caryatides stand with one knee bent, bearing the burden of the entablature with an appearance of ease and an absence of all strain. At times their flowing robes cling to their limbs, emphasising their roundness, at times they float free, giving an illusion of movement beneath. The Caryatides are one of the best-known European works of art, and are often quoted as the classic example of the alliance of function with freedom. To-day one sees the women of the south, carrying burdens on their heads, walking with just such a dignity. These stone maidens fulfil nobly their destiny as servants of the divinity, without sinking beneath the burden of a thousand years.

The finest piece of work done by the architect of the Erechtheum is the north portico. In its *90* details it resembles that on the east, except for a few slight variations, as, for example, in the plait above the upper torus at the base of the column. Here again the most subtle calculations have been *104* used. The columns have an entasis which is quite imperceptible and hardly even to be measured. The corner columns are slightly inclined towards the centre, the middle columns towards the interior and towards the south. After the vicissitudes that this building has been called upon to endure, its restoration is almost miraculous. The entablature, crowned by the cornice, runs almost without a break round three sides. Even the wall of the pediment still rises up, and the stone casket ceiling is in place, limiting the height of the wall. The richly ornamented door which leads into the *91* interior of the sanctuary invites us to enter. But we will remain here in the portico whose immensity, under this clear Attic sky, gives us a sensation of infinite peace.

The end of the Peloponnesian war brought about the downfall of the Athenian State. The Erechtheum was the last of the four great temples of the Acropolis. Other buildings without number have risen up beside them and disappeared. These alone have remained. In spite of their mutilated condition, they still stand, erect and eternal, as in the words of Demosthenes:

ΚΤΗΜΑΤΑ ΑΘΑΝΑΤΑ

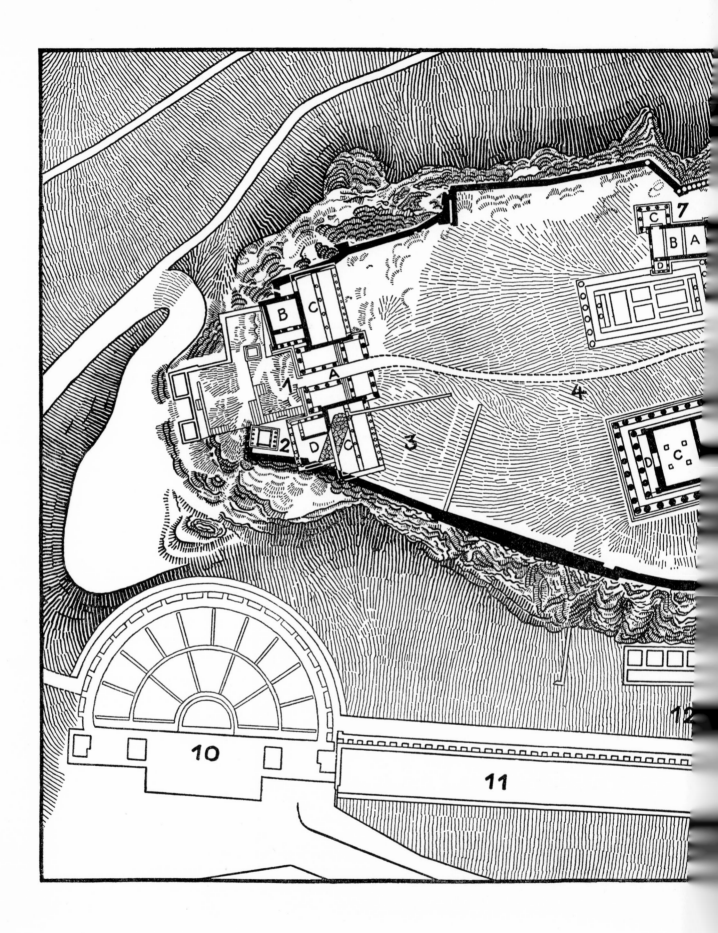

1. PROPYLAEA

    A Portico

    B Pinacotheke

    C Projected East Porticoes

    D Projected South-West Portico

2. TEMPLE OF ATHENA NIKE

3. PRECINCT OF ARTEMIS
    BRAURONIA

4. SACRED WAY

5. PARTHENON

    A Prodomus

    B Cella

    C Treasure chamber

    D Opisthodomus

6. TEMPLE OF ROME
    AND AUGUSTUS

7. ERECHTHEUM

    A Cella of Athena Polias

    B Cella of Erechtheus

    C North Portico

    D Caryatid Portico

8. EARLY TEMPLE OF
    ATHENA

9. MARBLE DRUMS BUILT
    INTO THE NORTH WALL

10. ODEUM OF HERODES
    ATTICUS

11. PORTICO OF EUMENES

12. ASCLEPIEUM

13. THEATRE OF DIONYSUS

I. TABLE OF PLATES IN THE TEXT

1. View from the roof of the Parthenon towards the site of the early Temple of Athena.

2. Lioness and young bull, from an early pediment.

3. Heracles and Triton from the pediment of the early Temple of Athena.

4. Typhon from the pediment of the early Temple of Athena.

5. Parthenon. East pediment. Drawing attributed to Carrey.

6. Parthenon. East pediment. Drawing attributed to Carrey.

7. Parthenon. West pediment. Drawing attributed to Carrey.

8. Parthenon. West pediment. Drawing attributed to Carrey.

9. Man bearing sacrificial calf.

10. Statue of young man (Early classical period).

11. Ionic female draped figure.

12. Ionic female draped figure.

13. The Acropolis in 1670 (From an original drawing in the Museum at Bonn).

14. Explosion of the Parthenon in 1687 (From a contemporary print by Fanelli in "Atene attica").

15. The Acropolis and the Frankish tower (From a contemporary sketch by the sculptor B. K. Heller, 1837).

16. The Acropolis in the 18th century (From Stuart and Revett, Antiquities of Athens, 1841).

17. Early cast of slab V, West Frieze.

18. Early cast of slab VIII, West Frieze.

The objects shown on Plates No. 2, 4, 9—12 are to be found in the Acropolis Museum. Photographs 1—4, 9, 10 were taken by Walter Hege; 11, 12 by the German Archaeological Institute in Athens.

II. TABLE OF PLATES

60

PROPYLAEA

58. Propylaea. West side.
59. Propylaea. East side.
60. Propylaea. Outer Portico.
61. Propylaea. Outer Portico and doors.
62. Propylaea. Outer Portico. Ionic columns and coffered ceiling.
63. Propylaea. Outer Portico. Side doors.
64. Propylaea. East Portico, looking westward through the doorway.
65. Propylaea. East Portico. View across to the Parthenon.
66. Propylaea. North-East corner of the central building.
67. Propylaea. South-East corner of the central building.
68. Propylaea. Capital from the outer Portico.

TEMPLE OF ATHENA NIKE

70. Temple of Athena Nike. North side.
71. Temple of Athena Nike from the Propylaea.
72. Temple of Athena Nike. East side.
73. Temple of Athena Nike. Balustrade. Nike untying sandal.
74. Temple of Athena Nike. Frieze and entablature on the East side, left half.
75. Temple of Athena Nike. Frieze and entablature on the East side, right half.
76. Temple of Athena Nike. Balustrade. Nike decking a trophy.
77. Temple of Athena Nike. Balustrade. Nike sacrificing bull.
78. Capital from the Parthenon, and Erechtheum.

ERECHTHEUM

80. View from the Parthenon towards the Erechtheum and the city of Athens.
81. Erechtheum. View from the South-West.
82. Erechtheum. View from the South-East, with the Hephaesteum ("Theseum") in the background.
83. Erechtheum. View from the South-East.
84. Erechtheum. East side.
85. Erechtheum. South wall and Caryatid Portico.
86. Erechtheum. View from the South-West.
87. Erechtheum. East side of North Portico.
88. Erechtheum. North-East corner, with the Parthenon and Hymettus in the background.
89. Erechtheum. South-East corner.
90. Erechtheum. North Portico.
91. Erechtheum. Door of North Portico.
92. Erechtheum. Caryatid Portico from the front.
93. Erechtheum. Caryatid Portico. View from the South-West.
94. Erechtheum. Caryatids.
95. Erechtheum. Caryatids.
96. Erechtheum. Caryatid on West corner, Side view.
97. Erechtheum. Caryatid on East corner, Back view.
98. Erechtheum. Frieze of the Cella wall.
99. Erechtheum. Frieze of the Cella wall.
100. Erechtheum. South-West corner of North Portico.
101. Erechtheum. Meeting-point of entablature and Cella wall.
102. Erechtheum. North Portico. Capital and entablature of central column. East side.
103. Erechtheum. North Portico. Capital and entablature of North-East corner.
104. Erechtheum. Bases of columns.

The photographs have been taken by Walter Hege, with exception of Nos. 20, 21, 42, 43, 49, 55, 56, 72, which were taken specially for this edition by Helga Schmidt-Glassner of Stuttgart and (No. 72) by Eva-Maria Czakó of Athens.

1. West side of the Acropolis, with the Propylaea and the Parthenon, in the afternoon sun

2. Acropolis, North side from Lycabettus

3. Acropolis, from the West, with the Areopagus and Lycabettus

4. Acropolis, South-East side, with the Olympieum in the foreground

5. The Parthenon and the Erechtheum rising above the South wall

6. Entrance to the Odeum of Herodes Atticus

The Odeum and the Portico of Eumenes

8. Aloes in flower on the western slope

10. Parthenon. West side.

11. Parthenon. North-West corner

12. Parthenon. Detail of South-East corner

3. Parthenon. North-East corner

14. Parthenon. South Portico, looking westward

15. Parthenon. South Portico, looking eastward

16. Interior of Parthenon, looking East

17. Parthenon. Treasure Chamber and West Door

18. Parthenon. Upper South-West corner

19. Parthenon. Upper North-East corner

20. Lapith and Centaur, metope from the South side of the Parthenon. London

21. Lapith and Centaur, metope from the South side of the Parthenon. London

22. Parthenon. West Frieze, view from the side

23. Parthenon. West Frieze, series of slabs with knights

24. Parthenon. West Frieze. Knight, marshal, and attendant

25. Parthenon. West Frieze. Youth and bearded man

26. Parthenon. West Frieze. Man on foot and horseman

27. Parthenon. West Frieze. Knight and man fastening sandal

28. Parthenon. West Frieze. Knights

29. Parthenon. West Frieze. Knight and rearing horse

30 Parthenon. West Frieze. Group of knights

31. Parthenon. West Frieze. Knights galloping

32. Parthenon. West Frieze. Youth

33. Parthenon. West Frieze. Youth and horse

34. Parthenon. West Frieze. Warrior fastening sandal

Parthenon. West Frieze. Knight

36. Parthenon. West Frieze. Horse with arched neck

Parthenon. West Frieze. Youth in broad-brimmed hat

38. Parthenon. South Frieze. Youth and horse

39. Parthenon. West Frieze. Head of bearded man

40. Parthenon. West Frieze. Rearing horse

41. Parthenon. West Frieze. Hind legs of horse

42. Parthenon. North Frieze. Group of knights. London

43. Parthenon. North Frieze. Youths and horses. London

44. Parthenon. North Frieze. Youths with sacrificial cows

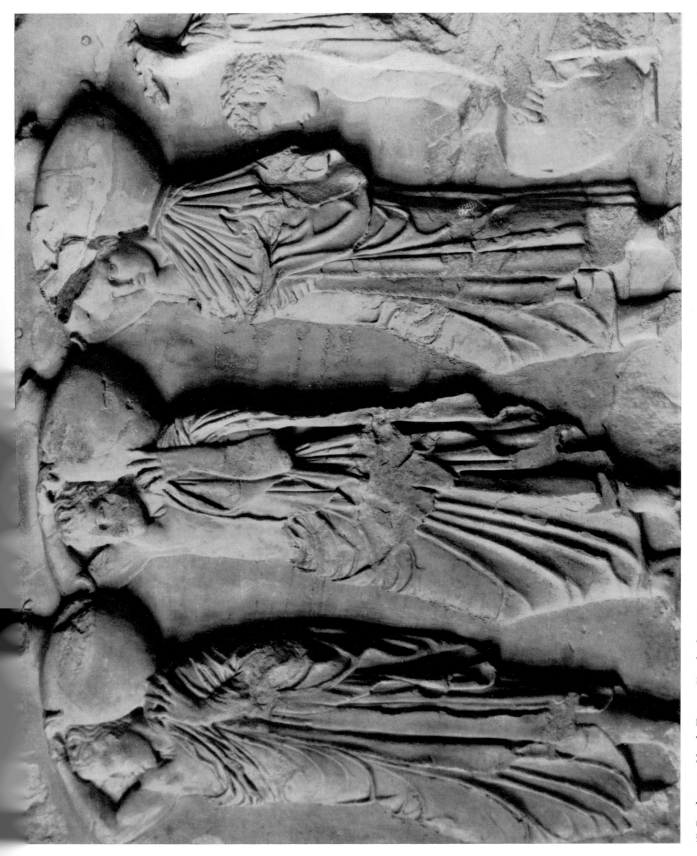

45. Parthenon. North Frieze. Youths bearing vases

16 Parthenon. North Frieze. Group of elders

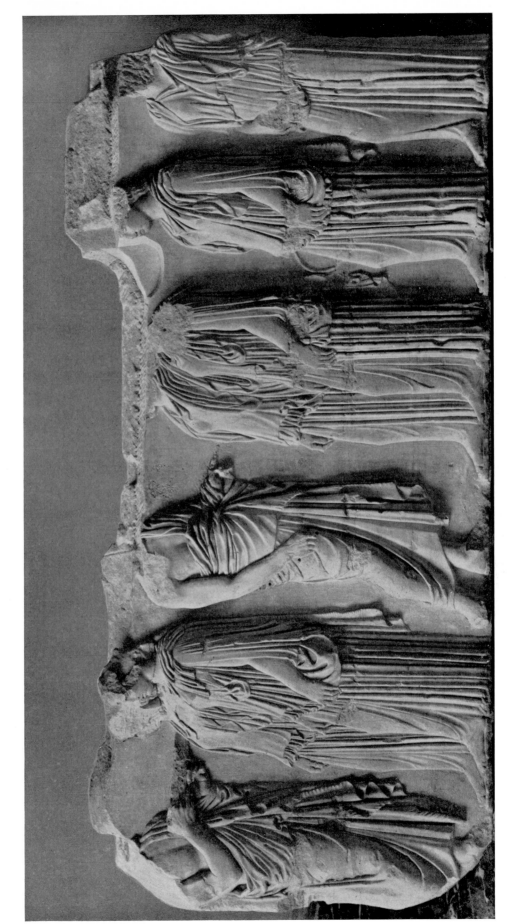

47. Parthenon. East Frieze. Group of girls with the masters of ceremonies

48. Parthenon. East Frieze. Poseidon, Apollo, and Artemis

49. Parthenon. East Frieze. Hera and Zeus. London

50. Parthenon. North Frieze. Youth

51. Parthenon. North Frieze. Youth bearing vase

52. Parthenon. East Frieze. Apollo

53. Parthenon. East Frieze. Artemis

54. Parthenon. West Pediment. Cecrops group

55. Parthenon. East Pediment. Deities. London

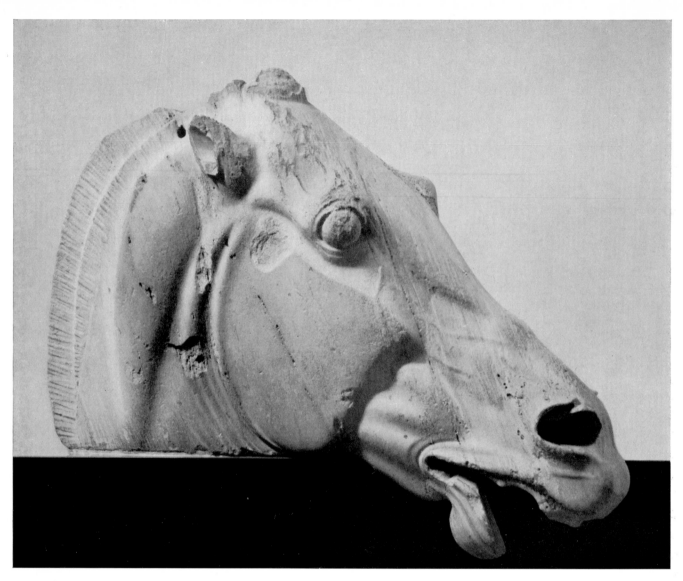

56. Parthenon. East Pediment. Head of horse. London

58. Propylaea. West side

59. Propylaea. East side

60. Propylaea. Outer Portico

61. Propylaea. Outer Portico and doors

62. Propylaea. Outer Portico. Ionic columns and coffered ceiling

3. Propylaea. Outer Portico. Side doors

64. Propylaea. East Portico, looking westward through the doorway

Propylaea. East Portico, view across to the Parthenon

66. Propylaea. North-East corner of the central building

67. Propylaea. South-East corner of the central building

68. Propylaea. Capital from the outer Portico

70. Temple of Athena Nike. North side

71. Temple of Athena Nike from the Propylaea

72. Temple of Athena Nike. East side

73. Temple of Athena Nike. Balustrade. Nike untying sandal

74. Temple of Athena Nike. Frieze and entablature on the East side, left half

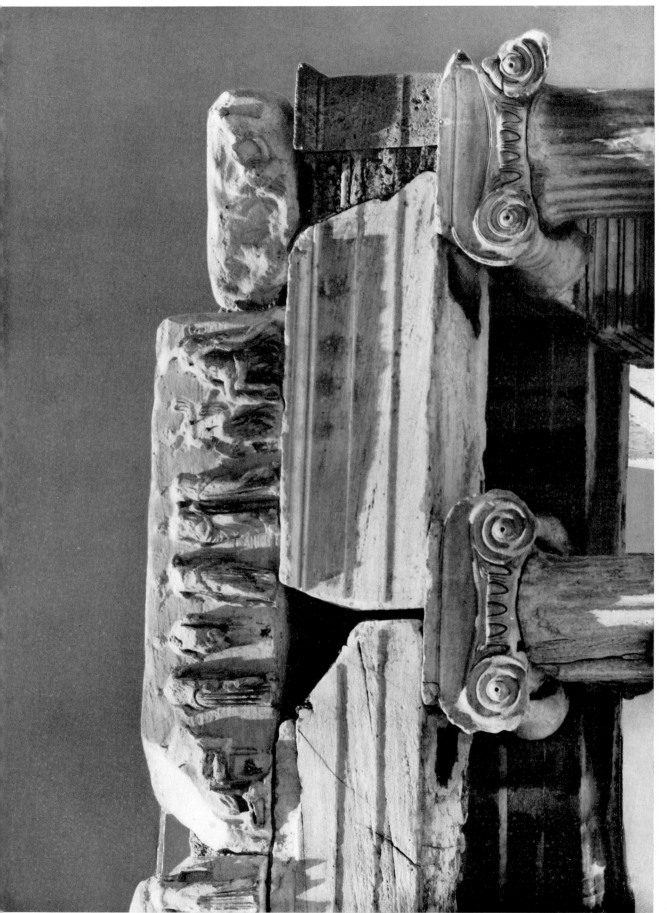

75. Temple of Athena Nike. Frieze and entablature on the East side, right half

76. Temple of Athena Nike. Balustrade. Nike decking a trophy

77. Temple of Athena Nike. Balustrade. Nike sacrificing bull

78. Capital from the Parthenon, and Erechtheum

80. View from the Parthenon towards the Erechtheum and the city of Athens

81. Erechtheum. View from the South-West

82. Erechtheum. View from the South-East, with the Hephaesteum in the background

83. Erechtheum. View from the South-East

84. Erechtheum. East side

85. Erechtheum. South wall and Caryatid Portico

86. Erechtheum. View from the South-West

87. Erechtheum. East side of North Portico

88. Erechtheum. North-East corner, with the Parthenon and Hymettus in the background

89. Erechtheum. South-East corner

90. Erechtheum. North Portico

91. Erechtheum. Door of North Portico

92. Erechtheum. Caryatid Portico from the front

93. Erechtheum. Caryatid Portico. View from the South-West

94. Erechtheum. Caryatids

5. Erechtheum. Caryatids

96. Erechtheum. Caryatid on West corner, Side view

97. Erechtheum. Caryatid on East corner, Back view

98. Erechtheum. Frieze of the Cella wall

99. Erechtheum. Frieze of the Cella wall

100. Erechtheum. South-West corner

101. Erechtheum. Meeting-point of entablature and Cella wall

102. Erechtheum. Capital and entablature of central column, East side

103. Erechtheum. Capital and entablature of North-East corner

104. Erechtheum. Bases of columns